THE JOURNAL OF
CORPORATE CITIZENSHIP

Issue 18
Summer 2005

Theme Issue: **Corporate Citizenship in Africa**

ISSN 1470-5001

Greenleaf PUBLISHING

THE JOURNAL OF CORPORATE CITIZENSHIP

General Editor Professor David Birch, Corporate Citizenship Research Unit, Deakin University, Australia

Regional Editors North America: Professor Sandra Waddock, Boston College, Carroll School of Management, USA; Europe/Africa: Professor Malcolm McIntosh, University of Bath, UK

Publisher John Stuart, Greenleaf Publishing, UK

Production Editor Dean Bargh, Greenleaf Publishing, UK

Book Review Editor Jerry Calton, University of Hawaii, USA

CORRESPONDENCE

The Journal of Corporate Citizenship encourages response from its readers to any of the issues raised in the journal. All correspondence is welcomed and should be sent to the General Editor via Boston College, Carroll School of Management, Chestnut Hill, MA 02467, USA; edjcc@bc.edu.

Entries for the **Diary of Events** should be marked '*JCC* Diary' and sent to journals@greenleaf-publishing.com.
Books to be considered for review should be marked for the attention of the Book Review Editor and sent to Jerry Calton, School of Business and Economics, University of Hawaii–Hilo, 200 W. Kawili Street, Hilo, HI 96720, USA; calton@hawaii.edu; notification should be also sent to edjcc@bc.edu.

• All articles published in *The Journal of Corporate Citizenship* are assessed by an external panel of business professionals, consultants and academics.

• *The Journal of Corporate Citizenship* is monitored by 'Political Science and Government Abstracts' and 'Sociological Abstracts'; and indexed in the Thomson Gale Business and Company Resource Center.

SUBSCRIPTION RATES

The Journal of Corporate Citizenship is a quarterly journal, appearing in Spring, Summer, Autumn and Winter of each year. Subscription rates for organisations are £150.00 sterling/US$250.00 for one year (four issues) and for individuals £75.00 sterling/US$125.00. Cheques should be made payable to Greenleaf Publishing and sent to:

The Journal of Corporate Citizenship
Greenleaf Publishing Ltd, Aizlewood Business Centre, Aizlewood's Mill, Nursery Street, Sheffield S3 8GG, UK
Tel: +44 (0)114 282 3475 Fax: +44 (0)114 282 3476 Email: journals@greenleaf-publishing.com.
Or order from our website: www.greenleaf-publishing.com.

ADVERTISING

The Journal of Corporate Citizenship will accept a strictly limited amount of display advertising in future issues. It will also be possible to book inserts. Suitable material for promotion includes publications, conferences and consulting services. For details on rates and availability, please e-mail journals@greenleaf-publishing.com.

Printed on acid-free paper from managed forests by The Cromwell Press, Trowbridge, Wiltshire, UK.

The Center for Corporate Citizenship at Boston College is the editorial and administrative home of *The Journal of Corporate Citizenship*. The Center's mission is to provide leadership in establishing corporate citizenship as a business essential, so all companies act as economic and social assets by integrating social interests with other core business objectives. The Center provides research, executive education, consultation and convenings on issues of corporate citizenship. For more information, visit www.bc.edu/corporatecitizenship.

THE CENTER
FOR CORPORATE
CITIZENSHIP
AT BOSTON COLLEGE

World Review

January–March 2005

A synopsis of the key strategic developments in corporate responsibility around the globe over the last quarter

Jem Bendell*   John Manoochehri†

Professionalisation: a new approach required

IN JANUARY THE INTERNATIONAL Organisation for Standardisation announced the establishment of a group to develop a global standard on social responsibility. The ISO Working Group on Social Responsibility will have its first meeting in March in Salvador, Brazil, aiming to set out a workplan culminating in the issue of standardised guiding principles for the field of social responsibility. This will represent an ISO reference for the business community to match its weights, measures, standardised grades of aluminium, and 15,000 other global standards. The development of this standard is the latest step in the growing 'professionalisation' of CSR service provision.

In addition to the development of standards for management practice, there are increasing moves to standardise the practice of those working in this field. At the end of last year AccountAbility and the International Register of Certified Auditors (IRCA) came together to launch the world's first individual certification scheme in the field of sustainability assurance. The so-called 'Certified Sustainability Assurance Practitioner Program' will help auditors—both internal as well as external to companies—provide quality assurance to sustainability reports.

This initiative came hard on the heels of a new CSR Academy in the UK, which developed a 'CSR Competency Frame-

* Adjunct Professor, Auckland University of Technology.
† Special Adviser, Stockholm Environment Institute.

ANDREW DUNNETT OF CSR ACADEMY:
PROMOTING THE 'CSR COMPETENCY
FRAMEWORK' FOR MANAGERS

work' for managers.[1] This outlines a set of core characteristics that CSR managers should exhibit, and is intended to help managers improve their skills both within the specific CSR profession and also in other specialisms where business–society issues are relevant. This is because 'in today's business environment,' says Andrew Dunnett of CSR Academy, 'managers across the business require the skills and competencies to take into account an increasing range and complexity of factors relating to the financial, environmental and social implications of business operations.'[2]

History teaches us of the mixed blessing when individuals and organisations come together to establish, improve and ultimately protect a profession. On the positive side, they provide the opportunity for people to share knowledge and expertise and maintain standards through peer review. They also provide a form of guarantee for consumers of professional services that the provider is of a certain standard, with particular training, qualifi-

cations and experience. However, this social benefit from professions and professional associations is not without its downside. 'Professions strike a bargain with society in which they exchange competence and integrity against the trust of client and community, relative freedom from lay supervision and interference, protection against competition as well as substantial remuneration and higher social status', commented the sociologist Rueschemeyer, some 20 years ago.[3] A body of work on the sociology of professions demonstrates that the definition of what is professional training, qualification, experience and practice is not just a technical exercise.

Some see professionalisation less as an issue of quality and more one of self-interest. 'All professions are conspiracies against the laity', wrote George Bernard Shaw in 1906. Today many regard the development of professions as projects of occupational closure. This means making it more difficult to get into the profession, thereby restricting supply of a service and driving up prices and remuneration. Professions can therefore play a role in perpetuating class divisions,[4] which could become a key issue for professionalisation in the area of business–society relations. Further, professionalisation of the CSR domain is likely to filter out the more creative wavelength of idea generation, to challenge fast-moving changes and weigh them with new administrative burdens, and to insulate itself from voices critical of the mainstream.

The history of professions also raises issues about the relationship of CSR and government. Professionals, whether accountants, doctors or others, have been found to seek and maintain the judgement domain and indeterminacy of their professional task as a way of empowering

1 See www.csracademy.org.uk.
2 A. Dunnett, 'Embedding CSR is the key to better performance', *Ethical Corporation*, November 2004.
3 D. Rueschemeyer, 'Professional Autonomy and the Social Control of Expertise', in R. Dingwall and P. Lewis (eds.), *The Sociology of the Professions* (London: Macmillan, 1983): 38-58.
4 T. Johnson, 'The Profession in the Class Structure', in R. Scase (ed.), *Industrial Society: Class, Cleavage and Control* (London: George Allen & Unwin, 1977).

their members, and also restricting external interference.[5] Thus professions seek a certain amount of independence from the state in order to carry out their activities; yet they need the state to give them a monopoly to protect their activities.[6] As the issue of public policies on CSR becomes more developed in subsequent years, so the relationship of the CSR profession to regulatory processes will become increasingly important. Evidently, an increasingly professionalised CSR community has a lot to lose by being critical of either its client base or regulatory masters.

Given that questions of organisational accountability are central to debates and initiatives on CSR and corporate citizenship, the accountability of CSR professionalisation must become a key issue. Who should CSR standards in development be accountable to? CSR practitioners? Or their intended beneficiaries? Can we assume that their intended beneficiaries are not only their clients but those affected by their clients' activities? If so, what opportunities for meaningful participation in CSR professional standards development can those constituencies really have? CSR professionalisation could learn well from the history of professions, as well as innovating a new conception of professional identity, where the professional serves not only the client but a set of principles that speak directly to the need for a more sustainable and just world.

Rethinking intellectual property

THE RESPONSIBILITY OF SOFTWARE companies towards society has not been high on the agenda of the corporate social responsibility community in recent years, perhaps because the environmental and social impacts of production appear to be very low, while the value added to society appears pretty high. When such companies as Microsoft appear in the corporate responsibility press it is often about traditional corporate philanthropy, involving their donation of products or services to specific educational projects.

However, information technology (IT) companies sit at the nexus of two of the most important changes to capitalism today, which should make them a key focus for future work on corporate responsibility issues. On one side is a key technological development in recent capitalism—cheap information technology—while on the other side is the international protection of intellectual property, which is probably the most important regulatory development in capitalism of our time, as it extends private property rights into new areas. The allocation of private property rights as opposed to collective use rights, and the responsibilities and obligations of those people or organisations that enjoy such property rights, is a key political question at the heart of capitalism. When the nature and allocation of private property rights are being negotiated, as is the situation with intellectual property today, it reveals to us the way 'property' is an inherently political concept concerning a balancing of private and collective interests. As this balancing of the private and collective interests is a key theme in most corporate social responsibility and citizenship debates, we might reasonably expect developments in the nature and allocation of property to appear.

The responsibility of pharmaceutical corporations who hold patents to crucial drugs for diseases such as AIDS has been the focus of some attention over the last few years. Most corporate responses have been in the form of cutting prices and in some instances relaxing their patents, to

5 N. Harding and J. McKinnon, 'User Involvement in the Standard-setting Process: A Research Note on the Congruence of Accountant and User Perceptions of Decision Usefulness', *Accounting, Organizations and Society* 22.1 (January 1997): 55-67.
6 E. Krause, 'Professional Group Power in Developing Societies', *Current Sociology* 49.4 (July 2001): 149-75.

improve access to medicines in the global South. However, the key issue of what constitutes the responsible use of corporate power in shaping the regulatory regime on intellectual property remains relatively undebated and unresolved. Recent events in the IT sector make this question even more urgent to explore, and bring IT companies more firmly into the corporate responsibility spotlight.

A significant development came in February, when the European Parliament rejected unanimously a draft Directive to introduce patenting for software.[7] The issue had been in play since moves in 1997/98 by the European Patent Office to institutionalise patents for software design, and on the negotiating table since a draft Directive was proposed in 2002.[8] The issue of patenting of software is just one of the intellectual property (IP) issues facing the information and communications technology (ICT) sector that have implications for public benefit, and thus can be considered in the context of corporate responsibility.

IP is legally defined under three headings: copyright, patents and trademarks. Patent coverage is generally more restrictive than copyright because, while copyright restricts re-use of a particular *piece* of creativity, a patent, in IP terms, is the equivalent of protecting a whole *style* of creativity. So, taking language as a hypothetical example, copyright covers a particular text; but patenting would cover a whole style of formatting, or genre of writing, or a certain use of grammar or punctuation. And, thus, applied to software, patents could impinge on a wide range of potential creativity, bringing all sorts of software developments within the scope of concepts of 'similarity' in both 'operation' and 'effect', and thus under the control of patent holders.

What is at stake here in practical terms? A huge amount for both business and society. The advance of open-source software has been rapid, with Linux, the desktop/server operating system, at the head of the charge. But the terrain onto which these newcomers are landing is not smooth, and is getting bumpier: the open-source movement is in serious danger of being tripped up not so much by questions of quality or compatibility (issues with open-source software that are now being overcome, partly through backing by computing giants such as Sun and IBM) but by questions over IP. If software patents are set up in Europe, the open-source movement might have its scope for software development badly curtailed; and Linux users are already being sued for illegally using, within the Linux software code, supposedly copyrighted proprietary code.

In 2004, Microsoft was bidding to install its software on the 14,000 desktops of the Munich municipal government. After eventually offering a 35% discount on the original US$40 million price tag and sending its senior management to meet the Mayor, the Munich government chose Linux, the freely available, no-licence-required open-source operating system for its desktop machines. This was a watershed decision. The Munich contract catapulted Linux from its ghetto in back-office servers to the mainstream via the desktop machines of a municipal government—a market where Microsoft's dominance has been hitherto unassailable.[9]

Nevertheless, the switch to Linux was nearly scuppered by the threat of messy IT patent lawsuits. Munich put its transfer to Linux on hold while it waited for a clarificatory ruling from the EU Commission over whether its shift to open-source would put it in regulatory difficulties should the then-current draft Directive on software patents have come into force; and leave it with software to which updates

---

7 'EU software patent law faces axe', *BBC News*, news.bbc.co.uk/1/hi/technology/4274811.stm.

8 'Software Patents in Europe: A Short Overview', swpat.ffii.org/log/intro/index.en.html.

9 B. Acohido, 'Linux took on Microsoft, and won big in Munich', *USA Today*, www.usatoday.com/money/industries/technology/2003-07-13-microsoft-linux-munich_x.htm.

would be only patchy and infrequent (since those updates would themselves be subject to patent disputes). In the end, Munich proceeded before receiving guidance—and Mayor Christian Ude told the Commission that it should scrap the software patents law in any case.[10]

Although the patent issue is on hold, at least in Europe, Linux is having a rougher ride in terms of copyright. Much of the crisis with Linux over copyright has arisen due to the company SCO, which claims that Linux uses some of its code (code for the parent system of Linux which SCO owns) illegally. SCO is therefore suing the biggest corporate users and vendors of Linux for colossal sums—firms such as IBM, DaimlerChrysler and computer companies such as Novell and Red Hat. The first sign of the strength of SCO's case, however, was revealed last year when a judge dismissed most of its case against DaimlerChrysler before a trial even commenced.[11] IBM, the biggest mainstream convert to Linux, having invested hundreds of millions of dollars in developing it for its machines and clients, has attempted to obtain a similar dismissal in its own lawsuit with SCO.[12] What may be working against SCO's claim that Linux has pirated code that it owns is its unwillingness to say which bits of code these actually are.

SCO's legal campaign poses difficult questions for Microsoft. This is because of the allegation from open-source advocate Eric Raymond, who analysed a leaked SCO email, that 'at least a third of SCO's entire market capitalization' comes from

MICROSOFT'S STEVE BALLMER, INTELLECTUAL PROPERTY RIGHTS WILL CAUSE DIFFICULTIES FOR THE GLOBAL SOUTH ADOPTING LINUX

Microsoft.[13] Despite various denials and clarifications, it appears that a significant commercial link may exist.[14] The question this raises is whether or not Microsoft's alleged association with SCO is a legitimate way to interact with its competitors. It also raises the issue of what is a responsible use of corporate power on issues as fundamental as determining the scope and nature of private property rights.

The probability of legal action, and its success, is not the same as the potential for legal action and it is the latter that concerns large corporations making long-term software decisions. Microsoft's Steve Ballmer, speaking late last year in India,[15] focused on the likelihood of continuing IP difficulties as the main risk posed for

10 J. Best, 'LiMux project moving again', *ZDNet UK*, news.zdnet.co.uk/software/applications/ 0,39020384,39163519,00.htm.

11 L. Rosencrance and T.R. Weiss, 'SCO Loses a Round in Court', *Computerworld*, www.computerworld. com/softwaretopics/os/linux/story/0,10801,94766,00.html.

12 'IBM Timeline: SCO Group v. International Business Machines, Inc.', *Groklaw*, www.groklaw.net/ staticpages/index.php?page=20031016162215566.

13 'Halloween X: Follow The Money', *Open Source Initiative*, 3 March 2004, www.opensource.org/ halloween/halloween10.html; M.J. Foley and S.J. Vaughan-Nichols, 'Leaked Memo Revives SCO–Microsoft Connection Furore', *eWeek*, 4 March 2004, www.eweek.com/article2/0,1759,1542915,00. asp.

14 C. Preimesberger, 'Analysis: Microsoft, SCO have a lot more explaining to do', *News Forge*, 8 March 2004, trends.newsforge.com/trends/04/03/08/0457259.shtml.

15 'Microsoft's Ballmer warns Asia against use of Linux', *India Times Infotech*, 19 November 2004, infotech.indiatimes.com/articleshow/928080.cms.

those in Asia deciding to adopt Linux. That copyright concerns are threatening the access of the global South to the software they need for their development is a concern, and the role of corporations in this situation should be legitimately considered as a question of corporate responsibility, especially given the increasing attention on corporate contributions to economic development in the South.

The main theoretical argument for the protection of software IP argues that properly protected IP is an incentive to perform ever better in a competitive environment: if you won't get any more from making even better products, because you can't protect the return on that investment, why make the products better? The fact that Linux is so successful without anyone having being paid to write its code suggests that this issue is open to debate. In addition, without serious competitors, protected IP becomes a licence to print money. The ethics of arguing about the need to 'protect return on investment from the competitive environment'—when there is no competitive environment—are problematic. In the absence of competition, the inevitable state of affairs is that profits are vastly in excess of investment—as they are in the case of Microsoft's products, running at up to 400% profit in some cases[16]—and that prices remain high with no incentive to come down. Poorer regions of the world should not be denied the opportunity to participate in development based on office and home computing; but, at current prices, they are.

Growing pressure from open-source technology and piracy led to Microsoft offering in February to sell its XP operating system at half-price across China, for a short period.[17] Microsoft has also

MICROSOFT SENIOR VP AND CEO OF EUROPE, MIDDLE EAST AND AFRICA, JEAN-PHILIPPE COURTOIS: BRINGING INFORMATION TECHNOLOGY TO JORDAN

responded to the 'digital divide' by rolling out a range of educational projects. Also in February, Microsoft senior vice president and chief executive officer of Europe, Middle East and Africa (EMEA) Jean-Philippe Courtois officially opened the Regional School Technology Innovation Center in Jordan, and announced Microsoft's collaboration with United Nations Development Fund Women's e-Village Initiative, to bring IT to educational centres across the country. 'Microsoft's alliance with the Jordanian Government is an extension of our broader commitment to help individuals, communities and nations in the Middle East region gain access to the technology, tools, skills and innovation they need to realize their full potential', said Mark East, Microsoft EMEA Senior Director of Education.[18]

The benefits of helping women to learn IT skills and have access to IT resources could be significant. However, is the best way of developing a sustainable IT sector

---

16 'Microsoft's money machine revealed', *The Inquirer*, 16 November 2003, www.theinquirer.net/?article=12694.

17 J. Chen, 'Microsoft cuts prices on China's market', *Shanghai Daily News*, 18 February 2005, english.eastday.com/eastday/englishedition/business/userobject1ai874791.html.

18 Microsoft, 'Progress on Microsoft Digital Inclusion Programmes in Jordan enables citizens to realise economic goals', press release, 22 February 2005, www.microsoft.com/middleeast/press/presspage.aspx?id=200522.

in countries such as Jordan to set people on a path of using proprietary software, rather than the free alternatives? One often-heard criticism of voluntary corporate responsibility initiatives is that they are part of a ploy to distract attention from systemic challenges by diffusing conflict. The business model of proprietary software companies appears inherently problematic for sustainable development, and so a true embracing of responsibility would be to look at how to change that business model.

Although Microsoft is a special case, other companies whose core business is based on digital IP protection could do well to engage in dialogue about the future of intellectual property. Security is so readily bypassed by the armies of crackers in the programming community, and files are so readily transferred online—often by 'centreless' peer-to-peer networks which cannot just be shut down—that some solution other than conventional IP enforcement may become commercially necessary, in addition to being more socially beneficial.

Rupert's rights

BEYOND THE REALM OF SOFTWARE, companies involved in information and communications technologies have been pushing for the introduction of new property rights. One example is 'The Draft Treaty on the Protection of Broadcasting Organisations', being negotiated at the World Intellectual Property Organisation (WIPO).[19] The proposed treaty aims to extend new rights to broadcasting organisations. This is not a category of society widely considered to be threatened by rights violations: last year Rupert Murdoch's News Corporation had amassed total assets of approximately US$53 bil-

DAVID TANNENBAUM OF THE UNION FOR THE PUBLIC DOMAIN: BROADCASTERS HAVE YET TO SHOW WHY NEW RIGHTS ARE NECESSARY OR DESIRABLE

lion.[20] The treaty would give such broadcasters, cablecasters and, under the US proposal, webcasters a range of new rights, and substantially expand both the scope and duration of currently recognised rights for broadcasting organisations.

The US National Association of Broadcasters (NAB) and the Association for Commercial Television (ACT) in Europe argue that new rights are a necessary measure to defend against 'signal theft', whereby a broadcast of a public event, for example, is picked up by a third party who re-broadcasts it. Lawyers for the Digital Media Association (DIMA) (whose members include AOL, FullAudio, RealNetworks and Yahoo) are arguing for the new protections to also include webcasters.

The extent of the re-broadcast problem remains open to debate. In addition, the draft treaty goes much further than signal protection, covering what happens when a signal has been received and stored. Such proposals could enable treaty broadcasters to restrict the distribution of material that is not copyrightable, is in the public domain or is made freely available by its creator. David Tannenbaum of the Union for the Public Domain argues that, while 'broadcasters have convincingly argued that the passage of this treaty will

---

19 WIPO, 'Revised Consolidated Text for a Treaty on the Protection of Broadcasting Organizations, Standing Committee on Copyright and Related Rights', Twelfth Session, Geneva, 17–19 November 2004, www.wipo.int/edocs/mdocs/copyright/en/sccr_12/sccr_12_2.doc.
20 'Corporate profile', News Corporation, www.newscorp.com/investor/index.html.

boost their profits', they have yet to show why the effort to create entirely new rights to the broadcasting stream is either economically necessary or desirable, particularly when balanced against its costs to society at large—such as restrictions on access to knowledge and encroachment on the public's rights to fair use.[21]

The draft treaty itself provides no justification for its existence in terms of the public interest. Thiru Balasubramaniam of the Consumer Project on Technology told *JCC* that social and development goals do not figure as issues to most participants in the WIPO committee that is drafting the treaty. That such issues are not a concern, let alone the top priority for WIPO, is highly problematic. As a UN agency, WIPO's work should be in support of the UN Charter, to advance peace and social progress. However, WIPO has struggled to understand its work in that context, and a coalition of 14 developing countries have called for the development dimension to be incorporated into the core of WIPO's mandate.[22] Others have questioned the impartiality of its secretariat, pointing to evidence that they have been pressurising governments to back the new treaty. 'It appears that the tail is wagging the dog', said Robin Gross of IP Justice. The institutional interests of WIPO and its closeness to industry may be key factors, which raises questions about appropriate corporate influence over intergovernmental institutions.[23]

As mentioned earlier, the nature of property rights, their potential extension, the social obligations of their owners, as well as the responsibilities of those who infringe such rights, should all be central to debates about corporate–society relations. Thus, the role of corporations in influencing the definition and regulation of private property should be a key focus for those concerned with corporations using their power more responsibly, for public as well as private benefit. However, a review of various online corporate social responsibility newsletters and magazines in the past months indicates that this has yet to emerge. Nevertheless, it is only a matter of time before companies such as News Corporation, Microsoft and Yahoo will need to consider more closely how the worldwide extension and consolidation of their property rights will impact on society, become more transparent about their political activities, and engage with their critics.

Is it good to talk?

THE MOBILE PHONE INDUSTRY IS another sector that, in conventional CSR areas of environmental impact and social responsibility, scores as low as the computing and software sectors as an industry of concern. Indeed, it is hailed as a sector that can catalyse social and economic development across the global South. But how *safe* is the technology? Is electromagnetic radiation a hidden pollutant? Recent debates in the UK highlight continuing concern about the relationship between science, politics, business and human health.

In January, the UK Health Protection Agency (HPA) issued updated guidance to the 2000 report of the National Radiological Protection Board (NRPB)—the 'Stewart Report'. 'Within the UK, there is a lack of hard information showing that the mobile phone systems in use are damaging to health . . . a precautionary approach to the use of mobile technologies should continue to be adopted . . . limiting the use of mobile phones by children remains appropriate as a precautionary measure.'[24] So that's clear then: Mobiles are safe. But use them with caution.

---

21 C. Deere, 'WIPO broadcasting treaty discussions end in controversy, confusion', *Intellectual Property Watch*, 22 November 2004, www.ip-watch.org/weblog/index.php?p=10&res=1024_ff&print=0.

22 www.cptech.org

23 C. Deere, *op. cit.*

24 Health Protection Agency, 'Documents of the NRPB, vol. 15 No. 5', www.hpa.org.uk/radiation/publications/documents_of_nrpb/abstracts/absd15-5.htm.

SIR WILLIAM STEWART, HEAD OF THE UK
HEALTH PROTECTION AGENCY: REPORT WAS
NON-COMMITTAL ON RISKS

The new report carries no specific limit for the age group of 'children' considered particularly at risk, but this did not stop one UK newspaper headlining its report on the updated study: 'No mobiles for under-nines, study says'[25] on the basis of ad hoc comments made by the head of the HPA, Sir William Stewart, at the press conference. Indeed the original Stewart Report was notably non-committal not just on the age of 'children' whose access to mobiles should be restricted, but also on what 'caution' really means in relation to the use of a mobile phone. Recommending 'shorter calls', as it did, is hardly a scientific breakthrough; and its other concrete recommendation, to use an 'approved hands-free set'[26] was contradicted by its own finding that no approved hands-free sets exist: 'The regulatory position on the use of hands-free kits and shields is unclear and the only information available to the public appears to be that supplied by their manufacturers.'[27]

The NRPB seems, in fact, to have overturned the conventional understanding of the 'precautionary principle', in that, rather than finding evidence for the safety of mobile technology, it states that mobiles are not known to be unsafe—but suggests 'caution' in any case. This may have gone unnoticed by the mobile-safety campaigners,[28] who point to more traditional interpretations—in which the burden of proof is on those wanting to implement a new technology, not on those against it. Perhaps the most important fact driving the NRPB's position is what the original Stewart report unashamedly stated: 'The use of mobile phones and related technologies will continue to increase for the foreseeable future.'[29] This really is clear: there is nothing we can do to stop it.

So who is driving the debate on mobile phone safety? The mobile phone networks, who on this issue now speak with one carefully honed voice—the media-savvy Mobile Operators Association (MOA)—immediately 'welcomed' the Stewart update.[30] Ditto the equally organised Mobile Manufacturers Association, emphasising specifically how NRPB has 'reaffirmed the absence of any scientific evidence of adverse health effects from wireless communications technologies particularly mobile phones'. Regarding the 'other end' of the mobile safety debate, the masts (or base stations), the MOA reminded us in February that the NRPB had stated 'there is no scientific basis for establishing minimal distances between base stations and areas of public occupancy'. And in their Corporate Social Responsibility reports for 2003/2004 both mmO$_2$ and Vodafone discussed these issues. Jim Stevenson, O$_2$'s Community Relations Manager, said 'we are building a lot less now than three years

25 M. Oliver, 'No mobiles for under-nines, study says', *Guardian Unlimited*, 11 January 2005, www.guardian.co.uk/mobile/article/0,2763,1387812,00.html.

26 'Summary and Recommendations', www.iegmp.org.uk/report/summary.htm, para. 6.75.

27 *Ibid.*, para. 6.88.

28 Tetra Watch, 'New research', www.tetrawatch.net/science/mthr.php.

29 'Summary and Recommendations', www.iegmp.org.uk/report/summary.htm, para. 1.2.

30 Mobile Operators Association, 'UK network operators welcome NRPB advice on mobile phones and health', 11 January 2005, www.mobilemastinfo.com/media/news/11_01_05.htm.

ago, but the level of community consultation is far greater today'.[31] The focus in its report is on the provision of reassurance and early information to the communities concerned. Vodafone, on the other hand, is more assertive in its dismissal of the scientific basis for community concerns over health. 'Based on current scientific review, there is no evidence of an impact on human health when electromagnetic fields (EMF) exposure levels are below internationally recognised guidelines', it stated.[32] So, as far as the mobile companies are concerned, caution notwithstanding, it's all systems go.

But these assertions by the mobile phone companies serve to amplify the inconsistency embedded in the Stewart report: that, if phones are safe, why is there any need to exercise 'caution'—indeed take any notice of the Stewart recommendations at all? Or, put in terms of the precautionary principle, if companies are aware that risks may emerge at a later stage, why are they not hesitating to put up masts and marketing their products with that risk in mind, rather than moving forward as though there will never be any health issues emerging from mobile telephony. The 'caution' that manufacturers are enacting amounts to either various forms of 'consultation', before doing what they plan, or leaving it to the consumers to decide their own fate. On the question of children's particular risk of exposure to electromagnetic radiation, the MOA confirmed in February simply that: 'the operators reviewed their marketing policies to ensure they do not actively market mobile phones to the under-16s', and the MMA explicitly passed the buck to parents, saying 'we believe that it is an issue of parental choice whether children should be provided with a mobile phone'.[33] And, in submitting a planning application near a school, the limit of their responsibility, according to the MOA is merely to follow governmental guidance and, in their own words, to 'provide evidence to the local planning authority that they have consulted the relevant body of the school or college as required by the guidance'.[34]

However calm the MOA and MMA are—and thus all the operators and handset manufacturers—about the issue of health, it refuses to go away. One claim, from the burgeoning mobile health action community but with strong scientific backing, is that the NRPB is, perhaps wilfully, measuring the wrong impact (studying only heating effects of microwave radiation, but not other effects, on the body).[35] Crucially, a Swedish/European study released in October last year, with the strongest scientific credentials,[36] suggested that, for users with more than ten years of regular mobile use, there was a clear link to cancers in the ear—acoustic neuroma—on the side of the head at which users normally held their phones. While the NRPB and mobile operators responded to a previous Swedish study, pointing out flaws,[37] they have notably failed to comment in depth on this latest Swedish research. And new health scares keep emerging. A Hungarian study last

31 *mmO_2 Corporate Responsibility Report 2004*, www.mm02.com/cr2004/downloads/7630_CORE_REPORT.pdf.

32 Vodafone Group plc, *Corporate Responsibility Report 2003/04*, www.vodafone.com/assets/files/en/CSR_Report_2003-04.pdf.

33 Mobile Manufacturers Forum, *Mobile Phones and Health 2004*, www.mmfai.org/public/docs/eng/MMF%5FViewpoint%5FNRPB%2Epdf.

34 Mobile Operators Association, 'Comment on certain issues raised in NRPB Mobile Phones and Health 2004 Report and media coverage', 1 February 2005, www.mobilemastinfo.com/media/issue_statements/01_02_05.htm.

35 www.cogreslab.co.uk

36 'Acoustic neuroma linked to mobile phone use', *Study in Sweden*, www.sweden.se/templates/SISResearchNews____10209.asp; F. Castellani, 'Mobile phone risk revealed', *News@Nature.com*, 14 October 2004, www.nature.com/news/2004/041011/pf/041011-11_pf.html.

37 www.nrpb.org

year argued a link between mobile phone use and low sperm counts.[38]

In the past there has been some suggestion of too close a link between the scientific research community and the mobile operators—for example, that NRPB funded 'independent' research from an adviser to Orange.[39] It remains the case that the main body funding 'independent' research on mobile phones and health, the Mobile Telecommunications and Health Research Programme (MTHR), is itself very considerably funded by the mobile industry itself.[40] Whether this arrangement faithfully implements the recommendation in the first Stewart Report that a 'substantial research programme should operate under the aegis of a demonstrably independent panel'[41] is open to question; and the mobile safety campaigners are not convinced.[42]

Nevertheless, many scientists with knowledge of the issues are becoming decreasingly convinced of just how safe mobile phones and masts are. March saw new research released suggesting that, finally, hands-free sets could be proved to reduce radiation reaching the head—if used with a ferrite bead that absorbed emissions from the cable itself. Lawrie Challis, head of the MTHR, was unequivocal: 'there is no evidence yet that mobile phones are harmful to health but people have not been using them long enough for us to be sure . . . Using a ferrite bead effectively reduces emissions to the head to zero but as yet manufacturers do not put them on hands-free kits . . . I am not sure why, but I wish they would . . . you

LAWRIE CHALLIS, HEAD OF THE MTHR: THERE IS NO EVIDENCE YET THAT MOBILE PHONES ARE HARMFUL

would think they would like to promote it.'[43] And the response from Michael Milligan of the MMF? 'I agree they can have an impact. But the bigger issue is that mobile phones are tested to comply with standards and have been passed safe.'[44] So, finally, we have a split between the UK scientific establishment on 'caution'— and the manufacturers. Stewart himself has been critical of the extent to which the manufacturers are using the precautionary principle in reverse (i.e. doing nothing until danger is proven). 'We said in the report that it's not possible to say categorically that there are not health effects. But what has come out from the industry is that mobile phones are safe', he said.[45]

The validity of the mobile phone industry's response to these issues through stakeholder dialogues is under question. At a MOA stakeholder meeting last year, at which government, industry and civil

---

38 L. Sherriff, 'Mobile phones rot your balls', *The Register*, 28 June 2004, www.theregister.co.uk/2004/06/28/mobile_ball_rot/; S. Boseley, 'Mobiles cut sperm count, says report', *Guardian Unlimited*, 28 June 2004, www.guardian.co.uk/print/0,3858,4957960-103690,00.html.

39 J. Griffiths, 'TETRA', *Ecologist*, October 2004, www.starweave.com/jays.

40 Mobile Operators Association, 'Mobile phone science review welcomed by industry', 14 January 2004, www.mobilemastinfo.com/media/news/14_01_04.htm.

41 Independent Expert Group on Mobile Phones, 'Report of the Group (The Stewart Report)', www.iegmp.org.uk/report/index.htm, para 5.270.

42 Tetra Watch, 'New research', www.tetrawatch.net/science/mthr.php.

43 'Bead "slashes mobile radiation" ', *BBC News*, 25 January 2005, news.bbc.co.uk/1/hi/health/4203077.stm.

44 *Ibid.*

45 L. Haines, 'Mobile phone industry in radiation risk rap', *The Register*, 13 September 2004, www.theregister.co.uk/2004/09/13/mobile_raditation_controversy [*sic*].

society stakeholders were present, many concerns were raised about processes of consultation. Some claimed that 'industry representatives often refuse to attend public meetings, and that this leaves communities feeling angry and disempowered' and that 'it was felt by some that the public get very frustrated that operators appear to be "judge and jury" on the health issue . . .'[46]

Other methods have been employed to understand stakeholder concerns. Vodafone commissioned a 'perception survey' from MORI in 2003 to assess public views of mobiles and mobile safety. That found 'the public believes that network operators are not taking the [radiation and health] issue seriously enough'.[47] Vodafone's response to this, as per its 2003/2004 Group CSR report[48] is that its 'role is to support independent research and explain the findings in plain language so that our customers have the information they need to make their own decisions on mobile phone use'. The message from the phone companies is that stakeholder engagement is not about listening to customers—it's about telling them everything's okay, according to the science. This is far from real dialogue—the irony being that phone companies might have something to learn about how to talk properly.

'It's important to abide by what the science tells us', said British Prime minister Tony Blair responding to a question on the subject of phones and sperm counts, in parliament last year.[49] Apparently, the science isn't telling us anything definitive either way. But if the trend of evidence, as the Swedish study on acoustic neuroma seems to imply, points to the pragmatic conclusion that mobile phone radiation does increase cancer risk, the deeper question is what anyone can or will do, and who will take the rap if things go wrong. The scientific community—led by Stewart and Challis—is starting to distance itself from the industry's calm. However, governments are making so much money from mobiles (the 3G licence auction brought in a staggering £22.5 billion to the UK government), they are not likely to want to slow the mobile juggernaut. If the evidence ever becomes overwhelming, it would appear that it will then be too late either to undo society's reliance on mobiles or to prevent a welter of health symptoms from arising due to long-term mobile use. If the precautionary approach ends up meaning everyone for themselves, then the mobile users themselves will end up being the scapegoats.

Whole-systems change

THE CASES OF MOBILE TELEPHONY and intellectual property in software and broadcasting illustrate the importance of regulation in shaping the market for new technologies and therefore the impact of such technologies on society. They highlight how the corporate influence on regulatory developments is a central question for corporate responsibility. The lack of engagement by the CSR community on these issues also highlights its limited engagement on the rules of the game—the system conditions that shape the environment within which corporations operate. However, in recent months the need for 'whole-systems change' in global capitalism, and the role of corporate leaders in helping this, has begun to be more widely discussed.

'Whole-systems change' means chang-

46 T. Greulich and R. Kemp, *Stakeholder Roundtable. Mobile Phones, Base Stations and Health: The Current State of the Issue*, 23 December 2004, www.mobilemastinfo.com/planning/stakeholder-roundtable-report-0303c_2vi.pdf.

47 Vodafone, 'Mobile Handsets and Health', www.vodafone.com/section_article/0,3035,CATEGORY_ID%253D3040602%2526LANGUAGE_ID%253D0%2526CONTENT_ID%253D232686,00.html.

48 Vodafone Group plc, *Corporate Responsibility Report 2003/04*, www.vodafone.com/assets/files/en/CSR_Report_2003-04.pdf.

49 *Hansard*, 14 July 2004, Column 1406.

ing the factors that shape what all agents within that system do. In the context of companies, this means changing those factors that shape what economic actors do, so that all behave in a sustainable and accountable manner. In January the introduction to *The Lifeworth Annual Review of Corporate Responsibility* called on CSR professionals to make their work 'a catalyst for systemic change', and outlined different paths that would together constitute a transformative CSR agenda.[50] Then the magazine *What is Enlightenment?* ran a special feature on 'The Business of Saving the World', which chronicled a nascent leadership among some business executives, aiming 'to transform the systems that govern global enterprise'.[51]

In the article Nike's Darcy Winslow identifies two system conditions that need to be tackled for all companies to be made more responsible. 'One is government: a lot of laws that are in place right now do not give financial incentive to do things differently in future. The other is Wall Street. At the end of the day, the shareholders and Wall Street are what keep corporations moving in the direction they are moving in.'[52] A few months earlier her company was the feature of an article in the widely read *Harvard Business Review*. In it Simon Zadek, CEO of the UK-based AccountAbility, chronicled the bumpy route Nike has travelled towards more responsible business practices. Organisations learn in unique ways, Zadek contends, but they inevitably pass through five stages of corporate responsibility, from defensive ('It's not our fault') to compliant ('We'll do only what we have to') to managerial ('It's the business') to strategic ('It gives us a competitive edge') and, finally, to what he describes as 'civil' ('We

SIMON ZADEK, CEO OF ACCOUNTABILITY: IDENTIFIED FIVE STAGES OF CORPORATE RESPONSIBILITY

need to make sure everybody does it').[53] This highest stage has strong resemblance to a whole-systems change approach.

Frank Dixon of Innovest Social Investors has noted that 'the traditional CSR movement has been focused on improving corporate environmental and social performance (i.e.: reducing pollution, making safe products, taking good care of employees, acting responsibly in developing countries, etc.). This has prompted great improvement, but much more is needed to achieve sustainability. The missing element of sustainability is system change.'[54] In the *What Is Enlightenment?* article he described Innovest's 'Total corporate responsibility (TCR)' approach to rating companies as one that 'recognises that economic and political systems essentially force firms to be irresponsible and unsustainable by not holding them fully accountable for negative impacts on society. TCR encourages firms

---

50 J. Bendell and W. Visser, 'Introduction', in *The Lifeworth Annual Review of Corporate Responsibility 2004* (www.Lifeworth.net, 2005).

51 E. Debold, 'The Business of Saving the World', *What is Enlightenment?* 28 (March–May 2005): 82; www.wie.org.

52 *Ibid.*, p. 88.

53 S. Zadek, 'The Path to Corporate Responsibility', *Harvard Business Review*, 1 December 2004; harvardbusinessonline.hbsp.harvard.edu/b02/en/common/item_detail.jhtml?id=R0412J.

54 F. Dixon, 'Total Corporate Responsibility: Achieving Sustainability and Real Prosperity', *Ethical Corporation*, December 2003; www.ethicalcorp.com.

to work proactively with others to achieve system changes that hold them fully accountable.'[55] TCR therefore suggests a new mind-set for business. Rather than seeing itself as one entity operating independently from the rest of society, business would see itself as being part of one interconnected system. It would give priority to the good of the overall system, and in so doing ensure its own prosperity. However, the TCR approach recognises the realities of today's marketplace and suggests that firms take practical, incremental, profit-enhancing actions that improve internal CSR performance as well as promoting system change. Other initiatives explicitly talking about systems change are the Global Transitions Initiative (GTI)[56] and Corporation2020, which asks the question, 'What would a corporation look like that was designed to seamlessly integrate both social and financial purpose?' In the first quarter of 2005 it continued its search by convening various experts to develop principles for the future corporation.[57] It is a major task, and whether it is able to provide some answers to systemic issues about the nature of property and profit, and then how to actually achieve the needed whole-systems change, is still to be seen.

The earlier discussion of corporate influence over governance on basic issues such as property rights and consumer safety illustrates that there is much work to be done for a systemic view to actually impact significantly on the global political economy. The most famous meeting of corporations and politicians, the World Economic Forum, in January, showed little evidence of a shift towards awareness of systemic problems and thus system-change solutions. WEF's recommendations for global priority-setting attended to some serious issues: poverty, equitable globalisation, climate change, education, the Middle East.[58] However, the recommendations were wedded to the usual neoliberal economic world-view of greater corporate activity being of benefit to all regions, including the poorer, and the limited role of governments in facilitating corporations' contributions by ever-'freer' international trade'.[59]

Perhaps we will require many more personal transformations before global transformations become possible. As the journalist for *What is Enlightenment?* put it, 'only as business leaders begin to fully embrace the truth of our unity and interdependence will they demand accountability from each other to change these powerful global systems'.

---

55 Debold, *op. cit.*, p. 89.

56 www.gtinitiative.org

57 forums.seib.org/corporation2020

58 World Economic Forum, *Global Town Hall Report*, 26 January 2005; www.weforum.org/pdf/AM2005/Global_Town_Hall.pdf.

59 World Economic Forum, 'Closing Plenary: What We Should Do in 2005', 30 January 2005; www.weforum.org/site/knowledgenavigator.nsf/Content/_S13543?open&event_id=1204&year_id=2005.

60 Debold, *op. cit.*, p. 89.

Prologue

I Am an African*

Thabo Mbeki

I am an African.

I owe my being to the hills and the valleys, the mountains and the glades, the rivers, the deserts, the trees, the flowers, the seas and the ever-changing seasons that define the face of our native land.

My body has frozen in our frosts and in our latter-day snows. It has thawed in the warmth of our sunshine and melted in the heat of the midday sun. The crack and the rumble of the summer thunders, lashed by startling lightening, have been a cause both of trembling and of hope . . .

My mind and my knowledge of myself is formed by the victories that are the jewels in our African crown, the victories we earned from Isandhlwana to Khartoum, as Ethiopians and as the Ashanti of Ghana, as the Berbers of the desert . . .

I am an African.

I am born of the peoples of the continent of Africa.

The pain of the violent conflict that the peoples of Liberia, Somalia, the Sudan, Burundi and Algeria suffer is a pain I also bear.

The dismal shame of poverty, suffering and human degradation of my continent is a blight that we share.

The blight on our happiness that derives from this and from our drift to the periphery of the ordering of human affairs leaves us in a persistent shadow of despair.

This is a savage road to which nobody should be condemned.

This thing that we have done today, in this small corner of a great continent that has contributed so decisively to the evolution of humanity says that Africa reaffirms that she is continuing her rise from the ashes.

Whatever the setbacks of the moment, nothing can stop us now!

Whatever the difficulties, Africa shall be at peace!

However improbable it may sound to the sceptics, Africa will prosper!

Whoever we may be, whatever our immediate interest, however much we carry baggage from our past, however much we have been caught by the fashion of cynicism and loss of faith in the capacity of the people, let us err today and say—nothing can stop us now!

Source: President Thabo Mbeki on the occasion of the adoption by the Constitutional Assembly of 'The Republic of South Africa Constitution Bill 1996'

---

* Formerly published in Rupesh A. Shah, David F. Murphy and Malcolm McIntosh (eds.), *Something to Believe In: Creating Trust and Hope in Organisations: Stories of Transparency, Accountability and Governance* (Greenleaf Publishing, 2003).

Corporate Citizenship in Africa

Introduction

Wayne Visser
International Centre for Corporate Social Responsibility, UK

Charlotte Middleton
National Business Initiative, South Africa

Malcolm McIntosh
Universities of Bath, UK, and Stellenbosch, South Africa

OVER THE PAST TEN YEARS, THERE have been immense changes sweeping the continent of Africa. While many of its people continue to be afflicted by war, poverty, disease and dictatorships, there have been considerable positive developments as well. Democracy and governance have been spreading, many economies have been growing at unprecedented rates and basic services have been extended to many of the continent's poorest populations. The 1990s saw the rise of a new generation of African leaders. Before 1990, appointments of national leaders tended to be characterised by military or party favour. In contrast, between 1990 and 1994, democratic leadership transitions took place in 11 countries. It is these new leaders, such as South Africa's President Mbeki, Nigeria's President Obasanjo and Senegal's President Wade, who have begun taking responsibility for Africa's economic recovery through initiatives such as Nepad (the New Partnership for Africa's Development) (Lundy and Visser 2003).

The effects of globalisation are also widely in evidence, with the fate of many businesses, including some of the world's largest multinationals, now inextricably linked with the fate of Africa. Similarly, corporate citizenship is enmeshed in the debate about Africa's future. In the context of Africa, we think of corporate citizenship as 'the role of business in a tripartite partnership with government and civil society in aiding development towards a more participative, rule-of-law-based society where basic human needs and rights are met'.

Arguably, Africa is the continent where the social needs are greatest. Life expectancy in Africa is still only 50 years on average (and as low as 38 years in some countries), gross national income per capita averages US$650 (and drops as low as US$90) and the adult literacy rate is less than 20% in some countries.[1] At the current pace of development, sub-Saharan Africa would not reach the Millennium Development Goals[2] for poverty reduction[3] until 2147 and for child mortality[4] until 2165; and, as for HIV/AIDS and hunger, trends in the region are heading up, not down (UN 2004).

Africa is also the continent that can claim to have benefited least from globalisation

---

1 2002 figures; World Bank 2004.
2 www.developmentgoals.org
3 Target 1: halve, between 1990 and 2015, the proportion of people whose income is less than one dollar a day; Target 2: halve, between 1990 and 2015, the proportion of people who suffer from hunger.
4 Target 5: reduce by two-thirds, between 1990 and 2015, the under-five mortality rate.

thus far. Indeed, many critics of globalisation claim that Africa has been actively excluded, historically exploited and unfairly discriminated against. Hence there is the possibility of Africa becoming a rallying point in the campaign of those who oppose the spread of neoliberalism in developing countries.

The track record of big business in Africa is mixed at best. There is certainly no shortage of examples of corporate complicity in political corruption, environmental destruction, labour exploitation and social disruption, stretching back more than 100 years. Equally, however, there is voluminous evidence of the benefits of business bringing capital investment, job creation, skills transfer, infrastructure development, knowledge sharing and social responsibility programmes to countries throughout Africa. The private sector remains one of the best-placed institutions to make a significant positive contribution towards improving social and environmental conditions in Africa.

What makes corporate citizenship in Africa not only fascinating, but also of critical importance, is that the continent embodies many of the most vexing dilemmas that business faces in its attempt to be responsible, ethical and sustainable: when do local cultural traditions take precedence over global standards and policies? How far do companies' responsibilities extend in dealing with HIV/AIDS? When does involvement in local governance become an unhealthy intrusion on the political process? How can business avoid creating a culture of entitlement and dependency through its charitable activities? Do global companies have a right to impose Western ideas of ethics on African societies that have their own, often different, sets of values? These present merely a sample of the wide-ranging issues of the African corporate citizenship landscape.

We may be familiar with issues on the corporate citizenship agenda, such as eradicating poverty, improving governance, tackling corruption, enforcing labour standards, protecting human rights, preventing resource depletion, controlling industrial pollution, ensuring environmental conservation, upholding business ethics and creating supply chain integrity. However, for many developed countries, these are hypothetical issues for philosophical debate; distant concerns happening across the ocean in another land. In Africa, they are 'in-your-face' issues that are a daily reality, an unavoidable part of doing business on this continent.

Academia has an important contribution to make in examining the complexities of corporate citizenship in Africa, in highlighting the meta-narratives and ideological tensions that underscore much of the debate, and in critically evaluating the progress (or lack thereof) by companies in their pursuit of social, economic, environmental and ethical goals. However, academic institutions and researchers focusing specifically on corporate citizenship in Africa remain few and under-developed.

The papers selected for this Africa special issue provide a tantalising vision of what this emerging academic movement could begin to deliver. The special issue kicks off with two Turning Point pieces which give a vivid insight into the complex challenges facing companies in Africa. The first, an interview with the Chief Executive of the South Africa Foundation, Michael Spicer, shows how a multinational with African roots views its corporate responsibility, while the second, by Mandy Rambharos, shares some of the lessons Africa's largest electricity provider has learned in responding to the HIV/AIDS pandemic.

A review of the emergence of corporate citizenship in South Africa over the past decade is provided from three different perspectives. Wayne Visser's paper focuses on the forces that have shaped corporate citizenship in South Africa and progress made by large companies since democracy in responding to the global corporate responsibility trends. In a fascinating complementary article, André Fourie and Theuns Eloff timeously review the impact of collective business action on the political, social and economic transformation that has occurred in South Africa over the last ten years. Daniel Malan cautions against blanket optimism enveloping the impact of South African companies in Africa, and introduces a typology that classifies companies—perhaps disconcertingly—as corporate citizens, colonialists, tourists and activists.

Several of the papers give insights into specific industry sectors: Ralph Hamann and his co-authors stress the critical importance of local governance systems, based on their experience of mining in Mali, South Africa and Zambia, while Niklas Egels highlights the dynamics of partnerships between business and civil society in the implementation of an electrification project in Tanzania. The articles by Catherine Dolan and Maggie Opondo on Kenya's cut flower industry, and Elliot Schrage and Anthony Ewing on Côte d'Ivoire's cocoa industry, both illustrate the benefits and limitations of multi-stakeholder standards and codes in shaping corporate citizenship behaviour. Finally, the paper by Derick de Jongh and Paul Prinsloo questions the adequacy of contemporary business education in preparing future leaders to deal with the paradoxes of corporate citizenship in Africa and makes suggestions for an alternative, critical pedagogy.

As guest editors, we hope not only that readers will both enjoy, and be challenged by, the stimulating content of this special issue of *The Journal of Corporate Citizenship* on Africa, but also that its publication will mark a change in the tide—a groundswell towards a more vigorous academic debate and robust research agenda on corporate citizenship in Africa.

References

Lundy, G., and W. Visser (2003) *South Africa: Reasons to Believe* (Cape Town: Aardvark Press).

UN (2004) *Human Development Report 2003* (Brussels: United Nations).

World Bank (2004) *African Development Indicators 2004* (Washington, DC: World Bank).

Wayne Visser is currently pursuing doctoral studies at the International Centre for Corporate Social Responsibility. His research is looking at 'meaning in the life and work of sustainability managers'. He is the author of *Beyond Reasonable Greed: Why Sustainable Business is a Much Better Idea* (with Clem Sunter; Human & Rousseau Tafelberg, 2002) and *South Africa: Reasons to Believe* (with Guy Lundy; Aardvark Press, 2002). Until 2003, he was Director of Sustainability Services at KPMG South Africa, where he continues as a special adviser. He is also the external examiner for the Sustainability Learning Network at the University of Cambridge in the UK. Wayne has a passion for Africa and the role business can play in helping the continent and its people realise their potential. He pursues his interests through writing, professional speaking and consulting.

✉ International Centre for Corporate Social Responsibility, Nottingham University Business School, Jubilee Campus, Wollaton Road, Nottingham NG8 1BB, UK

🖥 wayne@waynevisser.com

🌐 www.waynevisser.com

Charlotte Middleton manages the Sustainable Futures Unit (SFU) at the National Business Initiative (NBI) in South Africa, ensuring the SFU's work plays a catalytic role in sustainable development and strengthening leadership in the area of corporate citizenship. She leads the partnership between the NBI and the World Business Council on Sustainable Development and is on the Sustainability Committee of the Institute of Directors Southern Africa. She is also part of the South African interest group on the EFMD/UN Global Responsible Leadership Initiative. Charlotte edits the *BottomLine*, a publication dedicated to issues of sustainable development. She is currently completing her master's in Corporate Citizenship.

✉ National Business Initiative, 32 Prince of Wales Terrace, 3rd Floor, MPF House, Sunnyside Office Park, Parktown, 2193, South Africa

🖥 charlotte@nbi.org.za

🌐 www.nbi.org.za

Dr **Malcolm McIntosh** is Professor Extraordinary at the University of Stellenbosch's Sustainability Institute. He is a Special Adviser to the UN Secretary-General's Global Compact and co-editor with Sandra Waddock and Georg Kell of *Learning To Talk: Corporate Citizenship and the Development of the UN Global Compact* (Greenleaf Publishing, 2004). He is also author of *Raising a Ladder to the Moon: The Complexities of Corporate Social Responsibility* (Palgrave Macmillan, 2003). He was Founding Editor of *The Journal of Corporate Citizenship*, and is a former Director of the Corporate Citizenship Unit at Warwick Business School. He is currently Director of Envolve.co.uk, a UK-based sustainability action organisation, and is writing a book on *Deep Simplicity: How Small Thoughts Can Change The World*.

✉ 242 Bloomfield Rd, Bath BA2 2AX, UK

🖥 malcolm.mcintosh@btinternet.com

🌐 www.malcolmmcintosh.org

Turning Point

 ## Interview with Michael Spicer, Chief Executive, South Africa Foundation

Charlotte Middleton

National Business Initiative, South Africa

FOR THIS *TURNING POINT* ARTICLE, Charlotte Middleton met with Michael Spicer, who until the end of 2004 was Executive Director: Corporate Affairs at Anglo American and Executive Vice President of Anglo American plc. He is now Chief Executive of the South Africa Foundation, a non-executive board member at Anglo American and continues to consult to the company. They discussed various issues pertaining to operating as a multinational in Africa and what that means for corporate citizenship.

You have been a senior executive in Anglo American for many years. What has been your experience of how the notion of corporate citizenship (including social responsibility, business ethics and environmental sustainability) has changed over time?

The South African experience is unique: due to the environment that South African companies operated in during the apartheid years, they were naturally far more socially and politically active. They took an active economic and political interest in this country, demonstrating a

collective expression of this interest through the establishment of various institutions at the time. The Urban Foundation, for instance, looked at matters of housing, education and assisting with the eradication of influx control. The catalytic Consultative Business Movement played a valuable bridge building role, ultimately becoming the secretariat to the Convention for a Democratic South Africa (CODESA), which negotiated the democratic settlement in South Africa between 1990 and 1994—an enormous milestone in South Africa's journey to democracy.

Corporate social investment (CSI) in developed countries is typically more formalised; however, in South Africa it tends to be deeper and wider—it involves both the horizontal and the vertical dimensions. This has also been true of Anglo American Corporation. Its culture has been shaped by the founding family: a deep personal involvement and commitment to wider society. The initial CSI work of the company wasn't codified or professionalised; there was no textbook on how to do it.

This has changed, of course. With South Africa re-entering the global economy, companies listing on the London stock exchange, and global growth and maturation of the concept and practice of sustainable development, South African companies are approaching CSI far more professionally and systematically. People are now formally appointed to responsible and accountable positions—as opposed to ad hoc operations—and monitoring, reporting and evaluation is moving into line with global best practice. In fact, I think it is safe to say that, in some areas of CSI, South African companies take the global lead.

HIV and AIDS is clearly one of the biggest corporate citizenship challenges in Africa. Your company played a strong leadership role on this issue in South Africa. What can be learned from this experience by other companies?

From a CSI perspective, and particularly in the developing world, this issue is particularly interesting. The disease does not threaten an entire society and consequently business operations in the developed world, and therefore one does not need to completely change processes to deal with it. In South Africa it is of a totally different magnitude and order and therefore offers a unique study of business leadership responding to a major challenge.

Given the nature of the epidemic, the initial poor state of government policy, lack of statistics and the rapid evolution of the disease, it was hard to get a handle on it from a business perspective. Normally, with any business intervention there is a business plan, costing, risk assessment etc. before policy is set. In the case of HIV/AIDS it was impossible to do that at the beginning; there were just too many variables. Also there was a justified fear among the private sector that, by taking on the mantle of responsibility, government would abdicate, thereby creating an unmanageable burden for business.

And yet there were visionaries who made a leap of faith—recognising that, while the costs of involvement were high,

the ultimate cost for non-participation would be even higher. It took immense courage by individuals such as Anglo's Chief Medical Officer Brian Brink: courage that paid off when seen in relation to the catalytic role business played in leveraging commitment by government, business and global players—demonstrating that a vicious cycle can be made virtuous through the right intervention.

There are many lessons to be taken out of the experience: primarily that of leadership—the ability to go ahead even when peers are sceptical, as did Anglo's CEO. Second, that implementing a holistic policy requires long-term commitment and a very sustained and deep involvement. Third, there will be hurdles to overcome. Stigma, fear and other societal pressures make this process very difficult. However, with such a magnitude of responsibility, you cannot give up; you must keep going.

However, it must not be overlooked that, with limited capacity and resources for such an undertaking, while the private sector can make a huge difference, the state must ultimately come to the party in order for the work to be truly sustainable. Fortunately, in South Africa it is beginning to do so.

In the developing world, the juxtaposition of development needs and environmental concerns is most apparent. How do you see large multinationals operating in these contexts responding in the future?

Again one needs to take cognisance of the differences between developed and developing economies. One is post-industrial, which therefore requires the refining of a basic functioning economy. So, while there may be issues that are profound, you do not have to recreate the system. In the other case the economy is in a pre-industrial phase; is yet to be created. And of course the creation of a functional economy is a precondition for sustainable development. This was clearly shown at the World Summit for Sustainable Development: jobs, housing, infrastructure, water, sanitation, etc. were on top of the agenda rather than the finer elements of post-industrial concerns.

The challenge for multinationals is that they need to accommodate both. As sustainable development becomes more sophisticated and the business case built, it will be understood that sustainable development can go hand in hand with economic development. From a multinational point of view that is very exciting—an opportunity to bring that level of sophistication into the social and economic needs of broader society. One of my favourite concepts is that multinationals help 'thicken civil society' as a consequence of their operations and day-to-day needs.

What are the unique corporate citizenship challenges for multinational corporations operating in Africa? What would you say are some of the lessons about corporate citizenship to be learned from Anglo American's experience of investment and disinvestment in Zambia's copper belt?

The Zambia copper belt provides a good example of a multinational operating in the developing world. The reality is that a company needs to operate in a way which helps confront the broader societal needs such as housing, health, etc. but it needs to continue generating a profit to make this happen. Governments have to be sensitive to this.

The Zambia experience demonstrates the tragic consequences of nationalising and then comprehensively mismanaging a key industry over a period of decades. Unfortunately, the Zambian government relentlessly overestimated the value of a key asset, even once they had decided to privatise, making it difficult to privatise and turn around the situation. In the end, the basic business was unsustainable in prevailing economic circumstances—particularly for a multinational whose institutional shareholders had stringent requirements. Consequently Anglo exited with a great deal of pain for all parties.

The nature of stakeholder capitalism is challenging for developing-country environments where returns may be lower and time horizons longer, particularly if the state is weak and there is policy inconsistency and governmental interference. I still think there is quite a long debate to be had as to how the needs of multinational corporations and developing countries can be integrated into a mutually beneficially outcome.

Africa is often perceived by the rest of the world to have the lowest standards in terms of corporate citizenship (issues of poor governance, high levels of corruption, environmental impacts and lack of legal enforcement are often cited, for example). Do you agree with this perception? Are there examples of world-class corporate citizenship practices in Africa?

I don't agree that Africa across the board has the lowest standards of corporate citizenship. If one were able to systematically compare with Asia and Latin America, Africa would not be a noticeably poorer picture. Examples of AIDS programmes are certainly world-class. Collective initiatives in CSI in South Africa though organisations such as the National Business Initiative and the Business Trust have broken new ground, demonstrating a sophisticated corporate giving model in developmental terms.

Corporate citizenship and the role of business in promoting sustainable development are becoming increasingly high-profile and complex. What do you think should be the key priority areas for companies doing business in both the developed and developing worlds?

HIV and AIDS is of course a key issue, particularly in Africa. Community engagement is also a fundamental issue in terms of getting reciprocal understanding, between the needs of the community and how business can contribute and operate in a responsible way, and in turn generate understanding of the needs of the business to the local and broader community.

Ethics is another issue and I am not sure that 'ethical codes of conduct' are necessarily a panacea—they are often just words but not embraced and ingrained in the senior leadership nor indeed in the workers. Perhaps it is a case of too much form over substance? There is also the question of ethics in the sustainable development field itself. In systematising the industry, one must guard against this becoming a self-perpetuating set of activities where the real purpose is forgotten. It is therefore incumbent on business leaders, as well as practitioners, to subject themselves to scrutiny as to what is making a real contribution to responsible business conduct.

Turning Point

Managing HIV/AIDS at Eskom

A Non-negotiable for Business Sustainability

Mandy Rambharos
Eskom Holdings Ltd, South Africa

The impact of HIV/AIDS

There are an estimated 40 million people living with HIV, of which 26.6 million live in sub-Saharan Africa (Global Compact Learning Forum 2004). Since the start of the AIDS epidemic, 83% of all HIV/AIDS related deaths so far have taken place in Africa with the sub-Saharan part of Africa holding the majority of the world's infected individuals. In South Africa, the estimated prevalence is currently 4.7 million individuals.[1] Given these dire statistics, HIV/AIDS, undoubtedly, has a profound impact on the sustainability of the region.

Moreover, with more than 1,500 new HIV infections occurring every day, and over 50% of these in the 20–30 year age group, a worrying unknown for all organisations is the effect of this devastating disease on the country and consequently the sustainability of the organisations in the country.

Many African businesses or multinational businesses operating in Africa already have a competitive advantage because labour is often abundant and affordable.[2] Investors would look to invest in a country that has the most productive, lowest-cost workforce. Given the overwhelming effect of HIV/AIDS on the population, the competitiveness of sub-Saharan Africa, and by inference African businesses, is threatened. HIV/AIDS-related deaths lead directly to a reduction in the number of available workers of a productive age. As more inexperienced workers replace these workers, productivity may be reduced due to that initial lack of experience. This would often have a direct impact on profitability. Other, often hidden, impacts include strained labour relations, declining employee morale and mistrust between employee and employer.

Responses to HIV/AIDS

As an organisation currently conducting its business exclusively in South Africa and Africa, the containment and manage-

---

1 Eskom Management HIV/AIDS toolkit.
2 United States Agency for International Development, Washington, DC, www.usaid.gov.

ment of HIV/AIDS and its effects on its employees is a strategic priority for Eskom. Already:

▶ New infections are projected to cost Eskom four to six times the annual salary per individual infected.

▶ The annual costs of existing HIV infections during the period 2006–2010 will average 7% of the payroll (Fussler *et al.* 2004).

However, taking a long-term view, a business with appropriate HIV/AIDS-related programmes and policies in place should be able to avoid serious productivity losses and mistrust between employer and employees. The integration of such traditionally social issues into business planning underpins the philosophy of sustainable development. A workforce that is healthy in mind, body and spirit will translate into a healthy business.

Eskom has ensured that all employees, contractors, suppliers and customers are an integral part of Eskom's HIV/AIDS programme. The main objective of the programme is to minimise the impact of HIV/AIDS on both employees and the business. A set of programmes, with dedicated resources, has been formulated and implemented throughout the organisation. These are:

▶ **Information management**. Infrastructure has been established to help Eskom maintain a strategic focus on the developments related to the prevalence of HIV/AIDS in the business.

▶ **Self-awareness**. The level of self-awareness of HIV status among Eskom employees has been increased.

▶ **High risk**. High-risk areas and situations in the organisation for contract-ing HIV have been identified and are being addressed.

▶ **Communication**. A communication strategy to support the strategic management of HIV/AIDS has been developed and implemented.

▶ **Empowerment**. Steps have been taken to empower all employees with skills, knowledge and information to deal with HIV/AIDS effectively.

▶ **Care and support**. The programme caters for the psychological support of HIV-positive employees, the free treatment of sexually transmitted infections, and monitoring of TB[3] treatment.

▶ **Policies and practices**. The programme ensures that Eskom policies and practices do not discriminate against those that are HIV-positive.

No business operating in Africa is immune to the devastating impact of HIV/AIDS. Therefore a proactive stance towards HIV/AIDS management must be taken to retard the impact of the disease and ensure business sustainability.

Partnerships

The sharing of best practice and information is essential for continual improvement.

To this end, Eskom is a member of the Global Business Council (GBC) against HIV/AIDS. In addition Eskom chairs the Southern African Power Pool forum on HIV/AIDS. The main purpose of this forum is to share experiences and assist in capacity building. Eskom has also shared its experience with and assisted more than 20 companies in the country with infor-

---

3 It is estimated that 25% of the 160,000 tuberculosis (TB) cases in South Africa in 1996 were attributable to HIV. TB is therefore seen as the most common opportunistic infection and the biggest killer of people living with AIDS. TB is often the first AIDS-defining illness which changes a person's status from HIV infected to AIDS. By attacking the immune system, HIV makes a person 30 times more likely to progress from TB infection to TB disease (Eskom Management HIV/AIDS toolkit).

mation to help them start their own programmes. The Eskom HIV/AIDS programme has received two awards: for Business Excellence by the GBC and for the involvement of people with HIV/AIDS in the programme, including employing them as members of staff.

In an extremely important partnership dedicated to research on an HIV/AIDS vaccine, Eskom works with the Department of Health, Medical Research Council and Institute of Virology. The South African AIDS Vaccine Initiative (SAAVI), co-ordinated by the Medical Research Council, was set up to co-ordinate the research, development and testing of affordable and effective HIV/AIDS vaccines for southern Africa.

Where to from here?

Any business dealing with any threat would develop a robust plan to mitigate the threat quickly, affordably and responsibly. The impact of HIV/AIDS is no different. It can be managed effectively if approached in the same way as any other threat to a company's productivity and profitability.[4] Hence, a business needs to:

▶ Know the extent of the threat

▶ Identify key areas of intervention

▶ Set clear objectives

▶ Develop a plan of action

▶ Identify persons responsible for key activities

▶ Allocate a budget and other resources

▶ Continue to monitor and evaluate

The lessons learned from Eskom's experience suggest the following components of a successful HIV/AIDS programme:

▶ **HIV/AIDS strategy—planning for the future.** Explore the impact HIV/AIDS will have on the company and look at ways you can implement an effective HIV/AIDS strategy.

▶ **Learning materials—powerful weapons against AIDS.** There is a vast amount of information and resources to help a company to implement a comprehensive HIV/AIDS training and education programme in the workplace.

▶ **HIV/AIDS basics—adequate medical training.** Ensure the company has professional staff that understand HIV and AIDS—the virus, how it spreads, how the tests work and how the disease progresses over time.

▶ **Community projects—how to get involved.** With the HIV/AIDS epidemic increasingly taking its toll on human lives, communities are reaching out to the sick, the dying and the orphaned. Find out how the company can become involved in the community within which it operates.[5]

While this may seem financially onerous, when weighed against the potential impact of HIV/AIDS—both financial and societal—it is insignificant. Business exists within society and, as the adage correctly states: Business cannot succeed in a society that fails (WBCSD 2004).

References

Fussler, C., A. Cramer and S. van der Vegt (eds.) (2004) *Raising the Bar: Creating Value with the UN Global Compact* (Sheffield, UK: Greenleaf Publishing).

Global Compact Learning Forum (2004) 'HIV/AIDS: Everybody's Business', www.unglobalcompact.org.

WBCSD (World Business Council for Sustainable Development) (2004) 'Doing Business with the Poor: A Field Guide', www.wbcsd.org.

---

4 Eskom Management HIV/AIDS toolkit.
5 *Ibid.*

Mandy Rambharos's current role is to continually improve the sustainability profile of the organisation through the development and implementation of relevant sustainability strategies and policies which are guided by relevant national and international best practice.

✉ Corporate Sustainability (SHE), ESKOM Holdings Ltd, Megawatt Park, PO Box 1091, Johannesburg, 2000, South Africa

💻 mandy.rambharos@eskom.co.za

⊕ www.eskom.co.za

Corporate Citizenship in South Africa

A Review of Progress since Democracy

Wayne Visser

International Centre for Corporate Social Responsibility, UK

- Codes
- Corporate citizenship
- Globalisation
- Legislation
- Socially responsible investment (SRI)
- South Africa
- Stakeholders
- Sustainability reporting

This descriptive paper provides a brief overview of the emergence of corporate citizenship (CC) in South Africa since 1994. The paper is divided into three main sections: (1) the scope of academic research on CC in South Africa; (2) the main catalysts for the increasing focus on CC over the past decade in South Africa, including legislative reform, globalisation, stakeholder activism and codification; and (3) the general trend of CC in South Africa, including sustainability reporting and socially responsible investment. The paper concludes that South Africa has made significant strides towards maturity in CC practice.

Wayne Visser is currently pursuing doctoral studies at the International Centre for Corporate Social Responsibility. He is the author of *Beyond Reasonable Greed* (with Clem Sunter; Human & Rousseau Tafelberg, 2002) and *South Africa: Reasons to Believe* (with Guy Lundy; Aardvaark Press, 2002). Until 2003, he was Director of Sustainability Services at KPMG South Africa, where he continues as a special adviser. He is also the External Examiner for the Sustainability Learning Network (University of Cambridge, UK).

International Centre for Corporate Social Responsibility, Nottingham University Business School, Jubilee Campus, Wollaton Road, Nottingham NG8 1BB, UK

wayne@waynevisser.com

www.waynevisser.com

WHILE THE EMERGENCE OF CORPORATE CITIZENSHIP (CC) IN SOUTH AFRICA forms part of a wider global trend (McIntosh *et al.* 2002), there are a number of unique elements that have shaped the way in which the phenomenon has manifested and evolved in this country. The paper uses the concept of CC in the sense that Maignan and Ferrell (2000: 284) define it, as 'the extent to which businesses meet the economic, legal, ethical and discretionary responsibilities imposed on them by their stakeholders'. As Matten and Crane (2005) point out, this is essentially a reworking of Carroll's (1998) definition of corporate social responsibility.

With its reliance on secondary research and the awareness and experience of the author (based on six years as a CC consultant in South Africa and three years as a CC academic in the UK), this paper makes no claims to be either comprehensive, objective or to make an original contribution of primary research. Rather, the purpose of the paper is to present a picture of the development of CC as it has appeared to the author over the past ten or so years. Hence, despite presenting some positivistic, quantitative findings from research by others, the paper remains epistemologically interpretive and methodologically qualitative, employing a narrative style (Hughes 1990).

The paper aims to give some insight into the development of CC among large companies in South Africa: first, by looking at the scope of academic research existing on the topic; second, by examining some of the catalysts for the increasing focus on CC, including legislative reform, globalisation, stakeholder activism and codification; and, third, by reviewing some of the manifestations of the general adoption and practice of CC by large South African companies, as well as specific developments in sustainability reporting and socially responsible investment (SRI).

Scope of academic research

CC as an academic field of research in South Africa is a relatively new phenomenon. For example, the Corporate Citizenship Unit of the University of South Africa, which remains the only national academic institution with a dedicated focus on CC, was launched only in 2003. This may explain the relatively small number of academic papers on CC in South Africa.

Of the pre-1994 publications, most deal with the ethical investment issues relating to apartheid (Bond 1988; Lansing and Kuruvilla 1988; Paul and Aquila 1988; Di Norcia 1989; Paul 1989, 1992). Of the post-1994 articles, many focus on the individual ethics of South African managers (Roussouw 1994, 1997, 1998, 2000; Schwartz 1996; Morris *et al.* 1996; Van Zyl and Lazenby 1999, 2002; Abratt and Penman 2002). These fall outside of the scope of this paper, which focuses on CC at the corporate and national level over the past decade.

Some CC research has focused on specific South African sectors, most notably mining (Kapelus 2002; Hamann 2003; Hamann and Bezuidenhout 2003; Hamann *et al.* 2004) and chemicals (Acutt 2003; Acutt *et al.* 2004). Other areas have included SRI (Kumar *et al.* 2002; Sonnenberg *et al.* 2004), stakeholder theory (de Jongh 2004), CC in small and medium-sized enterprises (Jeppesen and Granerud 2004), corporate environmental sustainability (Visser 1999; Fig 2000), sustainability reporting (Visser 2002; Sonnenberg *et al.* 2004), corporate governance (Roussouw *et al.* 2002) and general CC (Post 2002).

These academic references will be further cited in the relevant sections below. However, it should be noted that by far the most comprehensive research conducted on CC in South Africa and cited in this paper has been by private, rather than academic, institutions.

Catalysts for change

Among the many possible catalysts for the development of CC, legislation, globalisation, stakeholder pressure and codification are often cited as drivers for change (Freeman 1984; Carroll 1999; McIntosh *et al.* 2002, 2004; Sethi 2003; World Economic Forum 2003; Leipziger 2003; de Jongh 2004). Although these are undoubtedly not the only factors to have influenced the CC agenda, they seem to the author to have been among the most significant. The following sections review each briefly in turn.

Legislative reform

The importance of legislation in the CC debate is widely acknowledged (Carroll 1999). However, in South Africa, the process of legislative reform since democracy has been especially significant. The policy framework for post-apartheid CC in South Africa was already implied in 1994 when the African National Congress (ANC) launched the Reconstruction and Development Programme (RDP). Apart from setting a broad tone for CC, the RDP also addressed specific issues in more detail, including poverty alleviation, environment, health, safety, workplace empowerment, affirmative action and human rights, all of which today comprise key elements of CC.

Many of these original policy aspirations became encoded in the Bill of Rights of the new 1996 Constitution, which set the remit for legislative reform to follow. Between 1994 and 2004, a wave of new legislation was enacted which had direct or indirect implications for CC. The most notable among these statutes are summarised in Table 1.

While poor enforcement due to lack of government capacity remains a serious challenge, legislation seems to have been an acknowledged driver for change. For example, in a KPMG (1997) self-completion survey by the largest 150 companies in South Africa, 83% cited government policy/legislation as the most significant pressure for greater environmental responsibility. More recently, however, the business case seems to have become a more dominant rationale for responsible business practice than legal compliance. In a 2003 survey of the Johannesburg Securities Exchange (JSE) top 300 companies, Trialogue (2004b) found that only 10% cited 'abiding by laws and regulations' as their one principal motivation for pursuing CC, compared with 38% who reasoned that 'it makes good business sense'.

Socioeconomic development	▶ Reconstruction and Development Fund Act (1994) ▶ Development Facilitation Act (1995) ▶ Mineral and Petroleum Resources Development Act (2002) ▶ Broad-based Black Economic Empowerment Act (2003)
Environment, health and safety	▶ Mine Health and Safety Act (1996) ▶ National Water Act (1998) ▶ National Environmental Management Act (1998) ▶ Air Quality Bill (2003)
Labour, governance and ethics	▶ Employment Equity Act (1998) ▶ Skills Development Act (1998) ▶ Promotion of Access to Information Act (2000) ▶ Promotion of Equality and Prevention of Unfair Discrimination Act (2000) ▶ Prevention and Combating of Corrupt Activities Act (2004)

Table 1 CC-RELATED LEGISLATION INTRODUCED BETWEEN 1994 AND 2004

Globalisation

Many of the current debates around CC relate to the impact of globalisation on developing countries (Scherer and Smid 2000; Scholte 2001; Held and McGrew 2003; Prahalad and Lieberthal 2003). Some of these argue that multinationals, as agents of globalisation, are responsible for declining social and environmental conditions in the emerging economies in which they invest, with CC representing little more than a public relations exercise to protect corporate reputations. Similar critical voices are common among the NGO and labour movements in South Africa, with groups such as the Alternative Information Development Centre, South African New Economics Foundation, Third-World Network (Africa) and Congress of South African Trade Unions being somewhat typical.

These critical perspectives should not be dismissed or ignored. Nevertheless, improvements in the CC practices of large companies since South Africa's re-entry into the international community in the 1990s have been evident. Partially, this seems to have been the result of a number of home-grown companies globalising and listing internationally, including, for example, Anglo American, BHP Billiton, Dimension Data, Lonmin, Old Mutual and SABMiller, and thereby being subject to much more rigorous corporate governance requirements and international scrutiny.

This in turn encouraged more extensive sustainability reporting among many of these multinationals in South Africa (although several local companies had been reporting on their environmental and social impacts for a number of years already). In addition, a number of these companies have followed the international trend of participating in stock market indexes which use various aspects of CC as criteria for selection, including, for example, the Business in the Community Indexes, FTSE4Good Global Index and Dow Jones Sustainability Index.

The impact of globalisation was also manifested when multinationals from abroad investing or reinvesting in South Africa instituted CC improvements at their local operations to be consistent with their international standards. Examples of which the author is aware from his own experience include the takeover of Sentrachem by Dow Chemicals, resulting in significant improvements in environmental, health and safety performance; the application of Levi's global policies on human rights and labour conditions to South African suppliers; and New Clicks being awarded the franchise for The Body Shop in South Africa, once it had met a range of strict ethical criteria.

Over the past ten years, the South African business community also got involved in various international CC-related initiatives, such as the establishment of a regional chapter of the World Business Council for Sustainable Development,[1] the Responsible Care Programme (for the chemicals industry), the development of the International Organisation for Standardisation (ISO)'s 14000 series, the United Nations Environment Programme (UNEP)'s Cleaner Production activities, the Minerals, Mining and Sustainable Development (MMSD) Initiative, the Kimberly Process (for diamond mining), the Global Reporting Initiative, the Global Business Coalition on HIV/AIDS, and the Johannesburg World Summit on Sustainable Development.

Stakeholder activism

While South Africa was among the first countries globally to acknowledge stakeholders in a corporate governance context (Roussouw *et al.* 2002), South African CC research using Freeman's (1984) stakeholder theory has been limited (Freeman 1984; de Jongh

---

1 Initially through the Industrial Environmental Forum, then BCSD: South Africa, and now the National Business Initiative (NBI).

2004; Hamann *et al.* 2004). Anecdotal evidence, however, suggests that stakeholder groups have become an important force for encouraging CC in South Africa. This has been manifested mainly through community groups challenging companies on whether they are upholding the constitutional rights of South Africa's citizens. Various landmark cases between 1994 and 2004 suggest that, although civil society still tends to lack capacity and resources in South Africa, this has been an effective strategy.

For example, in 1994, a series of mercury poisoning incidents and other alleged environmental malpractices by Thor Chemicals impacted negatively on the local community of Cato Ridge. The government appointed a Commission of Enquiry and eventually, in 1997, Thor paid a damages claim of R9 million (Visser 1999). In another case, in 1999, a judgement was passed in favour of the Save the Vaal Environment (SAVE) community organisation and against the Department of Minerals and Energy Affairs and Sasol Mining to prevent a coal strip-mine in close proximity to the Vaal River. The judgement rested on the lack of consultation with stakeholders before a mining licence was issued.

However, not all stakeholder engagement has been negative. There are numerous examples of a collaborative CC approach by business through organisations such as the Urban Foundation, the Business Trust, the National Economic Development and Labour Council (NEDLAC), the Southern African Grantmakers' Association (SAGA) and the National Business Initiative (NBI) (see, for example, Fourie and Eloff's paper in this issue). Other good benchmarks for an inclusive CC model in South Africa include the Community Awareness and Emergency Response (CAER) programmes in the chemicals industry, the adoption by companies such as SABMiller and British American Tobacco (BAT) of the AccountAbility (AA) 1000 standard's approach to stakeholder engagement, and business–NGO partnerships such as the Eskom–Endangered Wildlife Trust (EWT) and Nedbank–WWF projects.

Codification

The use of global standards and codes as a CC tool has mushroomed over the past ten years and South Africa has followed this trend (Leipziger 2003; Sethi 2003). While the debate still rages about the extent to which these standards and codes represent an adequate corporate response to the world's social and environmental challenges, they are nevertheless regarded as an indicator of CC practice (McIntosh *et al.* 2002, 2004). The research presented in this section covers standards and guidelines for environmental management systems (ISO 14001), corporate governance (the King Code) and sustainability reporting (the Global Reporting Initiative), which have been among the most influential on CC practices in South Africa.

ISO 14001

ISO 14001 has had a significant impact on the CC agenda among large companies in South Africa and continues to grow in influence. To begin with, in 1996 when the South African Bureau of Standards (SABS) launched the standard, it was the only one to offer local certification services. Today, it remains the largest certifier, with 245 ISO 14001 certifications by September 2004, but the list of competitors with a national presence now includes the British Standards Institute (BSI), Bureau Veritas (BVQI), Dekra, KPMG, NQA, PricewaterhouseCoopers (PwC), SGS and TUV. Various surveys by KPMG since give some indication of the patterns of adoption and reporting of ISO 14001 in recent years.

According to a KPMG (1997) survey of the top 150 companies in South Africa, nearly half (45%) of the respondents regarded awareness about ISO 14001 to still be 'low' at that time. A quarter (25%) were unaware of the details of the standard, while nearly a third (31%) were actively pursuing certification and a similar number (29%) were using it as a guideline but not planning to certify. In 1999, a survey of 60 companies with environmental management systems showed that 97% used ISO 14001 as their reference point, with 32% already certified, 41% intending to certify and the remainder intending to use the standard merely as a guideline (KPMG 1999a).

The King Code

In 1992, the Institute of Directors in Southern Africa (IoD) published the *King Report on Corporate Governance in South Africa*, introducing the notion of stakeholders into the business lexicon (Roussouw *et al.* 2002). When the IoD issued a revised and updated version of the King Report in 2002 (King II), they included a full chapter on integrated sustainability reporting, including the requirement that every company should report at least annually on the nature and extent of its social, transformation, ethical, safety, health and environmental management policies and practices (IoD 2002; IoD *et al.* 2002).

Although adoption of the code remains voluntary, the Johannesburg Securities Exchange (JSE) has subsequently made King II a listing requirement. The impact of this is clear in KPMG's (2004) survey of the 154 companies listed on the JSE's All Share Index, which shows that 65% now report annually on sustainability-related issues and 77% reference some form of internal code of ethics. Similarly, research of the JSE top 200 companies shows that nearly 60% claim to have already fully adopted the requirements of King II, while more than 90% claim they will fully comply in the future (Trialogue 2004b).

Global Reporting Initiative (GRI)

As one would expect, given the extensive referencing of GRI in King II and the fact that compliance with the King Code is now a listing requirement, the GRI Sustainability Reporting Guidelines are having a significant influence on CC in South Africa (Sonnenberg *et al.* 2004). Primary research among the JSE top 300 companies shows that more than 40% claim to be already using the GRI guidelines, while a further 50% claim that they intend to use them in future (Trialogue 2004b).

These figures may be inflated since, as of 9 September 2004, there were only 24 South African companies listed on the GRI's website as having declared their use of the guidelines. And only 19% of the top 154 JSE All Share Index companies mention the GRI Sustainability Reporting Guidelines in their 2003 annual reports (KPMG 2004). On the other hand, South African companies and stakeholder groups have shown leadership in spearheading the development of the GRI's guidelines for reporting on HIV/AIDS.

Trends

General CC

Research suggests that CC in South Africa developed from an initial focus on environmental responsibility, to an inclusion of health and safety, and social and economic issues (Post 2002; Visser and Sunter 2002). The findings of a KPMG (1997) survey give a good indication of the state of corporate environmental management in the mid-1990s in South Africa: 76% of the top 150 companies regarded the environment as a strategic priority, with 84% agreeing that the significance of environmental issues for the company would increase over the next five years. Trialogue's (2004b) survey of JSE top 300 companies on CC provides the most recent overview of business responsibility practices, showing today that all top companies (100%) claim CC is a priority, with 52% giving absolute priority status and 32% high priority.

One aspect of CC is corporate social investment, or philanthropy (Carroll 1999). Trialogue estimates that the total corporate expenditure on corporate social investment (CSI) in South Africa for the 2003 financial year amounted to R2.35 billion, 6.8% higher than in 2002. Based on the total CSI budget of a sample of 100 leading corporate grantmakers, the average CSI budget per company in 2003 was R13 million. In terms of the priority issues, education funding made up 39% of CSI spend in 2003, up from 35% in 2000, while spending on health (including HIV/AIDS) was up to around 10% in 2003, a similar proportion to support for job creation initiatives (Trialogue 2004a).

Sustainability reporting

The data compiled from KPMG's annual reporting surveys (KPMG 1998, 1999b, 2000, 2001, 2002, 2003) and presented in Table 2 gives a good impression of the emergence of corporate sustainability reporting as a trend in South Africa.

	1998	1999	2000	2001	2002	2003
Annual financial reports						
Environment	48%	49%	52%*	55%	49%	68%
Health and safety (including HIV/AIDS)	–	–	–	52%	40%	81%
Social/community investment	–	–	–	60%	45%	75%
Code of ethics/code of conduct	–	–	–	84%	87%	77%
Human capital development/training	–	–	–	81%	–	78%
Sustainability issues	–	–	–	57%	–	85%
Separate public reports						
Environmental, social or sustainability reports	–	–	–	10%	16%	20%

* Top 100 industrials

Table 2 SUSTAINABILITY REPORTING TRENDS BY THE TOP 100 COMPANIES IN SOUTH AFRICA

Despite the evident progress, especially since the launch of King II, South Africa still lags behind international trends. For example, the 16% of South Africa's top 100 companies that produced separate environmental, social or sustainability reports in 2002 is still significantly less than the 45% of the Global *Fortune* 250 companies and 28% of top 100 companies in 11 countries surveyed in KPMG's (2002) international survey. Similarly, the SustainAbility and UNEP (2000, 2002, 2004) global reporting surveys have tended to feature best practice South African companies that are the exception rather than the rule (e.g. Anglo American, BHP Billiton, Eskom, MTN Group, South African Breweries/SABMiller and Sasol).

KPMG's (2004) most recent survey, which covered the 154 JSE All Share Index companies, even suggests (when compared with the 2003 survey) that the trend of reporting on non-financial issues in South Africa may have reached its peak. The findings showed that 99 (64%) of these top companies provide some level of sustainability data within their public reports, of which 77 (50%) provide relevant data within their annual financial ('combined') reports, while 22 (14%) produce stand-alone social, environmental or sustainability reports. The report authors, however, caution that much of this reporting remains superficial.

Socially responsible investment (SRI)

The SRI trend in South Africa is well documented (Alperson 1995; Sonnenberg *et al.* 2004). In addition to featuring prominently in the SRI movement in the 1980s through the anti-apartheid disinvestment phenomenon, since 1992, South Africa has introduced more than 20 SRI funds nationally which track companies' social, ethical and environmental performance. According to research by the African Institute of Corporate Citizenship (AICC) (2002), the size of the South African SRI market in 2001 was approximately R18.6 billion, or 1.55% of the total investment market.

In a significant development, in 2002, South African legal and consulting firm Edward Nathan and Friedland launched a South African Sustainability Index which scrutinised and ranked the JSE top 40 listed companies based on sustainability criteria. In May 2004, the JSE launched its own tradable SRI Index, the first of its kind in an emerging market based on the triple-bottom-line approach of environmental, social and economic sustainability, underscored by good corporate governance.

Conclusions and implications

This paper has summarised some of the key areas in which CC among large companies has developed in South Africa since 1994. On several measures of CC, such as codification, corporate governance, sustainability reporting and SRI, there is evidence to suggest that significant changes have occurred. Examining the extent to which these initiatives have resulted in improvements in sustainability performance (e.g. reduced environmental impacts, improved health and safety records, better social conditions and more economic empowerment) was outside the scope of this paper and remains open to question, debate and research.

Other indicators of a CC-conducive environment, such as supportive legislation and active stakeholder engagement, are more ambiguous in their status. For example, although there has been progressive legislative reform, government capacity for enforcement remains a concern. Similarly, while there have been important cases of stakeholder activism, many community groups and civil society organisations still lack resources and capacity to actively engage with companies and vigorously defend their constitutional rights.

There are three main implications of this research. First, the paper relies heavily on surveys by a limited number of commercial institutions. Hence, there is a clear opportunity to improve the extent and accessibility of academic CC research in a South African context. Second, the constructive role of multinationals in bringing about social, environmental and economic improvements in developing countries, which this paper implies, adds to the academic and public debate about the effects of globalisation on development. Third, by highlighting areas of CC best practice and lagging performance, the paper suggests opportunities for the transfer of knowledge and learning between companies and countries.

Bibliography

Abratt, R., and N. Penman (2002) 'Understanding Factors Affecting Salespeople's Perceptions of Ethical Behavior in South Africa', *Journal of Business Ethics* 35.4: 269-80.

Acutt, N. (2003) *Policy, People and Petrochemicals: A Case Study of Voluntary Approaches to Corporate Environmentalism in the South Durban Basin* (unpublished PhD; Norwich, UK: University of East Anglia).

——, V. Medina-Ross and T. O'Riordan (2004) 'Perspectives on Corporate Social Responsibility in the Chemical Sector: A Comparative Analysis of the Mexican and South African Cases', *Natural Resources Forum* 28.4: 302-16.

AICC (African Institute of Corporate Citizenship) (2002) *Socially Responsible Investment in South Africa* (Johannesburg: AICC).

Alperson, M. (1995) *Foundations for a New Democracy: Corporate Social Investment in South Africa* (Johannesburg: Ravan).

Bond, K.M. (1988) 'To Stay or to Leave: The Moral Dilemma of Disinvestment of South African Assets', *Journal of Business Ethics* 7.1–2: 9-18.

Carroll, A.B. (1998) 'The Four Faces of Corporate Citizenship', *Business and Society Review* 100: 1-7.

—— (1999) 'Corporate Social Responsibility', *Business and Society* 38.3: 268-95.

De Jongh, D. (2004) 'A Stakeholder Perspective on Managing Social Risk in South Africa', *Journal of Corporate Citizenship* 15 (Autumn 2004): 27-31.

Di Norcia, V. (1989) 'The Leverage of Foreigners: Multinationals in South Africa', *Journal of Business Ethics* 8.11: 865-71.

Fig, D. (2000) *Towards a Research Agenda on Corporate Environmental Responsibility in South Africa: Moving beyond Apartheid, Embracing Compliance and Building Sustainable Systems* (Geneva: UNRISD).

Freeman, R.E. (1984) *Management: A Stakeholder Approach* (Boston, MA: Pitman).

Hamann, R. (2003) 'Mining Companies' Role in Sustainable Development: The "Why" and "How" of Corporate Responsibility from a Business Perspective', *Development Southern Africa* 20.2: 237-54.

—— and A. Bezuidenhout (2003) 'Case Study of Corporate Social Responsibility in the South African Mining Sector', paper presented at *Corporate Social and Environmental Responsibility in South Africa*, Johannesburg, 22 May 2003.

——, D. Sonnenberg, A. Mackenzie, P. Kapelus and P. Hollesen (2004) 'Corporate Citzenship, Collaboration and Local Governance as a Complex System: Lessons from Mining in South Africa, Mali, and Zambia', paper presented at the *Interdisciplinary CSR Research Conference*, Nottingham, UK, 22–23 October 2004.

Held, D., and A. McGrew (2003) *Governing Globalization: Power, Authority and Global Governance* (Cambridge, UK: Polity Press).

Hughes, J. (1990) *The Philosophy of Social Research* (Harlow, UK: Longman).

IoD (Institute of Directors) (2002) *King Report on Corporate Governance in South Africa* (Johannesburg: IoD).

——, KPMG and AES (2002) *Directors' Sustainability Imperatives: Best Practice Guidelines for 'Non-Financial' Matters* (Johannesburg: KPMG).

Jeppesen, S., and L. Granerud (2004) 'Does Corporate Social Responsibility Matter to SMEs? The Case of South Africa', paper presented at the *Interdisciplinary CSR Research Conference*, Nottingham, UK, 22–23 October 2004.

Kapelus, P. (2002) 'Mining, Corporate Social Responsibility and the Case of Rio Tinto, Richards Bay Minerals and the Mbonambi', *Journal of Business Ethics* 39: 275-96.

KPMG (1997) *KPMG–IEF Top SA Companies Environmental Survey 1997* (Johannesburg: KPMG).

—— (1998) *1998 Survey of Environmental Reporting in South Africa* (Johannesburg: KPMG).

—— (1999a) *1999 Survey of Environmental Management Systems in South Africa* (Johannesburg: KPMG).

—— (1999b) *1999 Survey of Environmental Reporting in South Africa* (Johannesburg: KPMG).

—— (2000) *2000 Survey of Environmental and Social Reporting in South Africa* (Johannesburg: KPMG).

—— (2001) *KPMG Survey of Sustainability Reporting in South Africa 2001* (Johannesburg: KPMG).

—— (2002) *KPMG International Survey of Corporate Sustainability Reporting 2002* (Johannesburg: KPMG).

—— (2003) *Integrated Sustainability Reporting in South Africa 2003* (Johannesburg: KPMG).

—— (2004) *2004 Survey of Integrated Sustainability Reporting in South Africa* (Johannesburg: KPMG).

Kumar, R., W.B. Lamb and R.E. Wokutch (2002) 'The End of South African Sanctions, Institutional Ownership and the Stock Price Performance of Boycotted Firms: Evidence on the Impact of Social-Ethical Investing', *Business and Society* 41.2: 133-65.

Lansing, P., and S. Kuruvilla (1988) 'Business Divestment in South Africa: In Whose Best Interest?', *Journal of Business Ethics* 7.8: 561-74.

Leipziger, D. (2003) *The Corporate Responsibility Code Book* (Sheffield, UK: Greenleaf Publishing).

Maignan, I., and O.C. Ferrell (2000) 'Measuring Corporate Citizenship in Two Countries: The Case of the United States and France', *Journal of Business Ethics* 28: 283-97.

Matten, D., and A. Crane (2005) 'Corporate Citizenship: Towards an Extended Theoretical Conceptualization', *Academy of Management Review* 30.1: 166-79.

McIntosh, M., R. Thomas, D. Leipziger and G. Coleman (2002) *Living Corporate Citizenship: Strategic Routes to Socially Responsible Business* (London: Financial Times Pearson).

——, S. Waddock and G. Kell (eds.) (2004) *Learning to Talk: Corporate Citizenship and the Development of the UN Global Compact* (Sheffield, UK: Greenleaf Publishing).

Morris, M.H., A.S. Marks, J.A. Allen and N.S. Perry Jr (1996) 'Modeling Ethical Attitudes and Behaviors under Conditions of Environmental Turbulence: The Case of South Africa', *Journal of Business Ethics* 15.10: 1,119-30.

Paul, K. (1989) 'Corporate Social Monitoring in South Africa: A Decade of Achievement, an Uncertain Future', *Journal of Business Ethics* 8.6: 463-69.

—— (1992) 'The Impact of US Sanctions on Business in South Africa', *Business and Society* 31.1: 51-57.

——, and D.A. Aquila (1988) 'Political Consequences of Ethical Investing: The Case of South Africa', *Journal of Business Ethics* 7.9: 691-97.

Post, J.E. (2002) 'The "Iron Law" of Business Responsibility Revisited: Lessons from South Africa', *Business Ethics Quarterly* 12.2: 265-76.

Prahalad, C.K., and K. Lieberthal (2003) 'The End of Corporate Imperialism', *Harvard Business Review* 81.8: 109-17.

Roussouw, G.J. (1994) 'Business Ethics in Developing Countries', *Business Ethics Quarterly* 4.1: 43-51.

—— (1997) 'Business Ethics in South Africa', *Journal of Business Ethics* 16.14: 1,539-47.

—— (1998) 'Establishing Moral Business Culture in Newly Formed Democracies', *Journal of Business Ethics* 17.14: 1,563-71.

—— (2000) 'Defining and Understanding Fraud: South African Case Study', *Business Ethics Quarterly* 10.4: 885-95.

——, A. Van der Watt and D.P. Malan (2002) 'Corporate Governance in South Africa', *Journal of Business Ethics* 37.3: 289-302.

Scherer, A.G., and M. Smid (2000) 'The Downward Spiral and the US Model Business Principles: Why MNEs Should Take Responsibility for Improvement of World-wide Social and Environmental Conditions', *Management International Review* 40: 351-71.

Scholte, J. (2001) 'Globalisation, Governance and Corporate Citizenship', *Journal of Corporate Citizenship* 1 (Spring 2001): 15-23.

Schwartz, M. (1996) 'Business Ethics in Developing Countries: A Response to Rossouw', *Business Ethics Quarterly* 6.1: 111-16.

Sethi, S.P. (2003) *Setting Global Standards: Guidelines for Creating Codes of Conduct in Multinational Corporations* (Hoboken, NJ: John Wiley).

Sonnenberg, D., M. Reichardt and R. Hamann (2004) 'Sustainability Reporting in South Africa: Findings from the First Round of the JSE Socially Responsible Index', paper presented at the *Interdisciplinary CSR Research Conference*, Nottingham, UK, 22–23 October 2004.

SustainAbility and UNEP (United Nations Environment Programme) (2000) *The Global Reporters* (London: SustainAbility).

—— and —— (2002) *Trust Us: The Global Reporters 2002 Survey of Corporate Sustainability Reporting* (London: SustainAbility).

—— and —— (2004) *Risk and Opportunity: Best Practice in Non-Financial Reporting* (London: Sustain-Ability).

Trialogue (2004a) *Corporate Social Investment Handbook* (Johannesburg: Trialogue).

—— (2004b) *The Good Corporate Citizen* (Johannesburg: Trialogue).

Van Zyl, E., and K. Lazenby (1999) 'Ethical Behaviour in the South African Organizational Context: Essential and Workable', *Journal of Business Ethics* 21.1: 15-22.

—— and K. Lazenby (2002) 'The Relation between Ethical Behaviour and Workstress amongst a Group of Managers Working in Affirmative Action Positions', *Journal of Business Ethics* 40.2: 111-19.

Visser, W. (1999) 'Greening the Corporates: The Transition, Local Business and Sustainable Development', *Development Update* 3.1: 65-76.

—— (2002) 'Sustainability Reporting in South Africa', *Corporate Environmental Strategy* 9.1: 79-85.

—— and C. Sunter (2002) *Beyond Reasonable Greed: Why Sustainable Business Is A Much Better Idea!* (Cape Town: Tafelberg Human & Rousseau).

World Economic Forum (2003) *Responding to the Leadership Challenge: Findings of a CEO Survey on Corporate Citizenship* (Davos, Switzerland: Global Corporate Citizenship Initiative, World Economic Forum).

The Case for Collective Business Action to Achieve Systems Change

Exploring the Contributions Made by the Private Sector to the Social, Economic and Political Transformation Process in South Africa

André Fourie
National Business Initiative, South Africa

Theuns Eloff
North-West University, South Africa

Much of the existing corporate citizenship literature focuses on the corporate citizenship efforts of individual corporations whose responsibility is presumed to extend beyond the core business to local communities and along the value chain. This paper argues that it is important to explore the potential for more fundamental impact on society through collective business action. Concrete evidence is presented that the private sector in South Africa has contributed to systemic transformation in unprecedented ways by promoting democracy, peace and sustainable development. While recognising the constraints of collective business initiatives, the potential of this more systematic approach to substantially increase the influence of the private sector may prove uncomfortable to those who oppose the growing power of business in public policy and global governance. There is a need to rethink the role of the private sector as one of the key players required to develop strategic responses to the complex sustainability questions facing the world in the 21st century.

- Business contribution
- Corporate citizenship
- Collective role of private sector
- South Africa
- Systems change
- Sustainable growth and development
- Public policy
- Democratic transformation
- Business and sustainability

André Fourie is the Chief Executive of the National Business Initiative (NBI) in South Africa. He was previously the founding managing director of Business Against Crime (BAC) and deputy executive director of the Consultative Business Movement. Academic qualifications include an MA (international politics) and MBA (Oxford Brookes University).

National Business Initiative, PO Box 294, Auckland Park 2006, JHB, South Africa

andre@nbi.org.za

www.nbi.org.za

Theuns Eloff is the Vice-chancellor of the North-West University in South Africa. Eloff previously headed the NBI and the administration of South Africa's national constitutional negotiations. He holds bachelors' degrees in law and theology, and a master's and doctorate in theological ethics.

North-West University (Potchefstroom), Private Bag x6001, PU for CHE, Calderbank Ln, Potchefstroom, 2520, South Africa

rktte@puknet.puk.ac.za

www.nbi.org.za

THIS PAPER EXPLORES THE COLLECTIVE CORPORATE CITIZENSHIP CONTRIBUTION of the private sector during South Africa's democratisation process. This experience demonstrates that it is in the vested interest of corporations and broader society for business leaders to consider strategies that go beyond the conventional role of business and contribute towards building peace and shaping a stable society.

The extraordinary contribution of the private sector to the ending of the apartheid system and a peaceful transition to a democracy is not well documented in academic journals. The involvement of the business sector in facilitating the political process, mediating between the major political parties and eventually in electoral support for the country's first ever democratic election in 1994, must be recognised as a major contribution to the democratisation process and a unique role for business in the world (*Financial Mail* 1994: 20-21). As such, this paper aspires to making a contribution to the academic corporate citizenship literature by methodically documenting this evidence. The paper is deliberately positive in its perspective (rather than critical) of the contribution business has made to social transformation in South Africa.

The bulk of current corporate citizenship literature deals with the various facets of the corporate citizenship challenges faced by individual corporations such as impact on the natural environment or local communities, and taking responsibility for impact along the corporate value chain. It is argued here that it is important to recognise and understand the potential for more fundamental impact on societies through business coalitions. Insufficient attention has been paid to the potential systemic impact of business through co-operative action.

Corporate citizenship: a framework for analysis

The corporate citizenship framework has emerged as one of the leading approaches to shape and understand the broader role of business (Corporate Citizenship Unit 1998: 3-11; Corporate Citizenship Company 1999: 2-9). The paper employs a wide definition of corporate citizenship, incorporating business's contribution to peace, democracy, housing, safety, education and job creation.

Based on a thorough review of the corporate citizenship academic literature, Fourie (2002: 37-38) concluded that there is insufficient focus on the role the private sector can play in terms of public policy dialogue and engaging the state productively. This paper will focus on a neglected aspect of corporate citizenship: namely, public policy dialogue and engagement. This refers to the public policy role of business in the broader social sphere and excludes the well-documented role of corporate lobbying for direct company or industry benefit. The basic argument here is that transparent engagement with public agencies and regulators by the business sector can assist with social policy in areas such as education, economic development, employment, environmental issues and training (Nelson 1996: 7-9). Policy choices regarding public housing, education and welfare will shape development and the operating environment for years to come and are thus of primary importance to business (Whittaker 1996: 6-10).

It is argued that this gap in the literature provides the scope for a potential contribution by this study to the academic debate about corporate citizenship. A useful contribution to this debate was the recent study by SustainAbility and the UN Global Compact (2004) to explore the limits of individual corporate social responsibility. The study stated that individual efforts by companies run the risk of being too isolated from the core business and not being connected to the wider systems to make a major impact. The South African business sector's collective contribution to the country's transition will be used to contribute to this emerging paradigm.

The South African case study

This section provides a selective overview of the role of the private sector during the South African transition process as a basis for analysis. The evidence selected draws heavily on the role of the Consultative Business Movement (CBM) and its successor organisation the National Business Initiative (NBI). Clearly, there were many other contributions by the private sector (both positive and negative). But, for the sake of informing the debate about the collective role of business during a transition period, this was deemed the most appropriate focus, not least due to the authors' past and present involvement in these organisations, and hence their intimate knowledge of the contribution they have made.

The peace process

The business sector was frequently criticised during the late 1980s for the fact that major corporations were perceived to have supported and benefited from the apartheid system. This argument, which certainly cannot be dismissed out of hand, nevertheless does not pay sufficient attention to the noteworthy role played by a small group of business leaders to promote peace and democracy (Hofmeyr and Chapman 1994: 2). At that time, a small group of business leaders initiated a series of meetings with the (then apartheid) government and a wide range of formal and informal political groupings; including black political leaders who enjoyed mass-based support. The primary purpose was to encourage debate on the political and economic future of the country. Progress was hampered by the repressive political climate and the fact that many of the political leaders were either in hiding, detention, jail or exile. Despite these challenges, the relationship building initiative continued and in late 1988, following a high-level meeting between business leaders and representatives of the Mass Democratic Movement in Broederstroom, the Consultative Business Movement (CBM) was formed (CBM 1997: 8-12). The initial focus was on consultation and relationship building with all the key political players such as the African National Congress (ANC) and Inkatha Freedom Party (IFP). This was particularly significant given that it was at a time when broad trust was non-existent in the country.

The 1980s was a very turbulent and violent period in South Africa, with high levels of political violence across the country. The need for a national peace conference was undeniable. However, the political dynamics and power struggle between the government and ANC (and some of the other parties) presented a complicated problem regarding who had the power to convene such a conference. The National Party (NP) Government's effort to convene an official national peace conference was opposed by the liberation movements on the basis that the government was seen as a primary instigator of violence. The impasse was broken when, through a combined effort, the CBM and South African Council of Churches (SACC) facilitated a process that led to an inclusive peace process. The first meeting of the formal peace process was convened at the offices of Barlow Rand Ltd, a leading industrial company. The meeting was co-chaired by John Hall (Barlows executive and Chairman of the Chamber of Commerce) and Archbishop Desmond Tutu. This was the start of a long process in which business leaders played an active (but by no means exclusive) part in working with political parties, women's groups, religious groupings, NGOs and labour unions to foster a climate of peace (Hall 2004: 1-3; Eloff 2004: 2).

Democratic transformation and consolidation

The credibility and legitimacy of the CBM was established during the peace process and laid the foundation for the organisation to be asked to provide the secretariat and administrative support for the Convention for a Democratic South Africa (CODESA) process (Fourie 2004: 3). When the CODESA process deadlocked in 1992, the CBM convened local academics and foreign experts with the 'passive approval' of the major political parties in an effort to break the deadlock in constitutional negotiations about powers of the regions versus the central government. The resulting report played a critical role in the thinking of the major parties and proved to be decisive in shaping the final constitutional agreement on this politically sensitive issue (Friedman 1994: 168-69).

With less than a month to go before the first democratic elections, the IFP was refusing to participate in the elections. After Nelson Mandela suggested international mediation, the CBM was requested to manage a process to secure international mediation of the situation. Dr Henry Kissinger and Lord Carrington were leading figures in the international delegation that arrived in South Africa ten days before the scheduled election. When the mediators failed to reach a common agreement with all the parties on clear terms of reference, the prominent international mediators left the country. An informal shuttle diplomacy process was started by one of the lower-profile international mediators with intense support from the CBM. A corporate jet was used to secure buy-in from the IFP leader Buthelezi, (then President) F.W. De Klerk and (then ANC leader) Nelson Mandela (Friedman and Atkinson 1994: 38-39; Coleman 2004: 4; Spicer 2004: 1-2). This agreement formed the basis for the first democratic elections in the history of South Africa.

During 1993 the CBM facilitated the formation of the Business Election Fund as a dedicated mechanism to mobilise business support for a free and fair election. The institution launched a major national media campaign to promote democratic values and to support an inclusive election process. The mere fact that the business sector was publicly calling for a democratic election was seen by some as a political stance by the private sector. However, the campaign took great care to remain non-partisan while striving to project confidence regarding the future of the country with its slogan 'Business stands for building a great nation'. Other activities included a major voter education campaign in rural areas and a range of practical and logistical efforts to support the Independent Electoral Commission (*Financial Mail* 1994: 20-21; Business Election Fund 1994: 1-9; Hofmeyr and Chapman 1994: 10).

The following sections outline further examples of collective business action to pursue social aims since the country's democratisation.

The National Business Initiative

In 1995, a year after the country's first democratic election, business leaders initiated the amalgamation of the Urban Foundation (UF) with the CBM, resulting in the establishment of the National Business Initiative (NBI). The objective was to demonstrate the renewed commitment of the private sector to a new, democratic South Africa. The NBI was formed as a not-for-profit, public-interest and business-based organisation, dedicated to reconstruction and development in the country. The NBI stated from the start that it aims to tackle systemic problems, ensuring that there is national impact at scale. The organisation stated that it aims to work in partnership with government by mobilising business and management skills to address public issues, to facilitate the business community's collective contribution in the reconstruction of South Africa and to build constructive relationships and trust between government and business (Eloff 2001: 2).

Business Against Crime

In 1996 nearly 500 business leaders met at the World Trade Centre in Johannesburg to deliberate on how the private sector could contribute to the fight against crime in South Africa. Following intense dialogue with (then President) Nelson Mandela, a new organi- sation called Business Against Crime (BAC) was established to partner with the govern- ment in dealing with this major threat to safety and security in the new democracy (*Financial Mail* 2000a: 10-12). The NBI facilitated this process and served as the man- aging agency of BAC until the organisation was eventually set up as a separate legal entity. This new non-profit organisation provided support to many industry-specific responses to crime including those by the banking, tourism, computer and motor sectors. BAC also provided analysis, conceptualisation and planning skills for the integration of the crimi- nal justice system, including the required IT infrastructure, identification services and integrated case management (NBI 1995/1996: 5; BAC 2004).

Housing Delivery Task Team

The NBI was approached by the Department of Housing in 1996 to assist with the delivery of housing aimed at assisting the Government of National Unity to meet the 'housing for all' challenge. The NBI established the Housing Development Support Team (comprising businesses) to improve the delivery system. Major attention was paid to fixing the information management and the management systems, as well as reducing unnecessary bureaucratic delays and building the capacity of provincial officials. This effort resulted in capital subsidies awarded to first-time homeowners rising from 220,000 in 1996 to over 1 million by August 1999. At this stage the NBI began prepara- tions for handing back the management of the systems to the relevant national and provincial housing authorities (Eloff 1999: 8; NBI 2000: 10-12).

Colleges Collaboration Fund

The NBI played a leading role in mobilising the private sector in South Africa to appre- ciate the importance of further education and training (FET) colleges in meeting the skills and employment creation needs of the country. Over R80 million has been invested in restructuring the FET sector and building leadership and management capacity in the colleges. The NBI helped in shaping the policy for FET and subsequently formed the Colleges Collaboration Fund to partner with the government for the implementation of the system transformation. Key focus areas included repositioning the previously neglected FET system as a desirable option for students, expanding the overall headcount enrolments, securing a growth and diversification in programmes, a more equitable staff equity profile and exposing senior college staff to global best practice through an international exchange programme (NBI 2003: 18-19; CCF 2004: 7- 11).

Business Trust

In 1998 a grouping of business leaders and organisations co-operated to undertake intense discussions with the government on the challenges of economic growth and job creation. A firm foundation of the initiative was the broader concern among leading business people about unemployment. An important outcome of the dialogue was the formation of the R1 billion Business Trust, a five-year project designed to focus on the creation of jobs and building human capacity. An early key focus was to develop a stronger business approach to the international tourism marketing of the country, as a basis for sustainable job creation. The private sector worked with the public sector in appointing senior business representatives to the board of a restructured SA Tourism, developing a sophisticated market segmentation strategy and implementing a value-for- money business plan. By 2002, South Africa was the world's fastest-growing tourist destination, international tourist arrivals having increased by 20.2% (*Financial Mail* 2000b 9-10; Brink 2000: 2-3; Business Trust, www.btrust.org.za).

Key lessons

From the above discussion it is clear that the role of the private sector during the South African transition period and beyond has been exceptional. The rest of this paper will explore the corporate citizenship lessons from this experience and the implications for other societies.

The importance of business leadership

Business leadership proved to be an essential element in each of the major business contributions described. It took great courage and personal risk for the first business leaders to engage with the ANC and the banned political leaders within apartheid South Africa. They had to deal not only with the threats of a repressive regime but also received little support from fellow business leaders (Hofmeyr and Chapman 1994: 1-3; CBM 1997: 1-2). Leadership was also a critical dimension in the slightly unusual interventions (for a business sector) such as Business Against Crime and the Business Trust.

Two additional facts are striking. First, there is consistency in the leadership in the various initiatives and some individuals played a leading role in virtually all the business contributions. Second, it is often a small group of business executives taking the lead and early risk. They usually succeed in convincing a broader group of business leaders and the programmes are then sold as being supported by the entire business community. This may be true in the end, but it is worth recognising that it often takes only a few courageous leaders to initiate fundamental change.

The imperative of reciprocal political leadership

None of the interventions described above could have been achieved by the business sector alone. It is simply not well placed to re-engineer a country's criminal justice system or negotiate a political settlement and new constitution. It takes political courage to expose the business sector to the insides of a dysfunctional criminal justice system and to partner with relative strangers to rebuild a politically sensitive function that is core to government's mandate. According to the NBI (2000: 1-4), government support and co-operation at all levels are vital in the implementation of any public–private partnership. In short, without government commitment these types of interventions are simply not possible.

The power of the collective

Collective business efforts do have comparative advantages over individual company efforts in particular areas. An obvious efficiency benefit is the pooling of scarce resources (people, leadership and financial) towards a common end. SustainAbility and the United Nations Global Compact (2004: 30-31) stress the importance of reaching scale and critical mass, by moving beyond the potential impact of any individual corporation. Additional benefits of a collective approach include the need to deal with suspicions that a particular company may be aiming to gain individual advantage, demonstrating a common commitment to the broader national interest and managing the risk of companies being singled out for criticism on sensitive issues (Fourie 2004: 1).

Building responsive institution

It is striking to observe the wide range of institutions developed by the private sector to deal with particular issues. Some of the more prominent institutions mentioned in this paper include the Urban Foundation (dealing with the reality of African urbanisation within a system of apartheid influx control), Business Against Crime (helping to address crime and violence), the Business Election Fund (mobilising business resources for the first democratic election), the Business Trust (building trust and engaging the unemployment challenge) and the NBI (demonstrating business commitment to the new South Africa). These specialised agencies are set up on a dedicated basis to manage specific challenges and often closed when they have fulfilled their purpose. On the other hand, there is a great deal of continuity in the both the business leadership and executives employed.

Beyond projects: systems change and policy impact

The case study demonstrates that a variety of methods and approaches were used to achieve the desired results. Different situations clearly demand different approaches. The most prominent approaches noticed in the South African case include process facilitation, policy impact, programme management and institutional strengthening. Although it must be accepted that the responsibility for the formulation of public policy ultimately rests with the public sector, this is the key domain for achieving systems impact. The contestation of public policy in an emerging democracy is desirable but somewhat untested in terms of the role of business in shaping social policy. It is generally accepted that business has a legitimate right and responsibility to influence such policy where there is direct impact on the company or industry such as tax policy, industry regulation and competition policy. The role of business in influencing broader social policy is much less well understood.

Building trust and relations

A unique role by the private sector was the provision of process and secretariat services to the multi-party constitutional negotiations such as the CODESA and the Multi-Party Negotiation Process (MPNP). In hindsight it is necessary to ask how the CBM was trusted as a business organisation to provide administration services to the constitutional negotiation process. It is evident that this privilege was not easily granted but earned through years of relationship building, and informed by the constructive role played by business in the peace process (Fourie 2004: 3). Although a key consideration was the ability of the CBM to be recognised as a credible and professional non-partisan organisation, it must be accepted that it would have been possible to identify other parties to provide professional administrative services. Trust was a key ingredient for the business-based organisation to be used to render the organisational and process services necessary for the MPNP (Eloff 1999: 5-6). The ability of the business sector to remain non-partisan was thus essential for the political players to allow it to play such a support function (Ramaphosa 2004: 4).

Limitations of business coalitions

This paper has demonstrated beyond doubt that the private sector can play a meaningful role in effecting systems change for both the public good and shaping the broader environment in which it has to operate. However, it is important to retain a sense of perspective regarding the scope and potential for business impact. The power of major corporations to influence politicians or shape public policy is often overestimated by outside observers. Despite the lack of academic literature on this subject there is a need to consider some of the key limits to the potential for business coalitions:

▶ Corporations are competitive by nature and not inclined to co-operate with other corporations and particularly not with direct competitors. There must thus be a limit to how much they are prepared to invest in co-operative ventures where the benefits accrue to broader society rather than individual companies.

▶ Perceptions of undue influence are almost inevitable in a situation where many are sceptical of the power and influence of major corporations. Regardless of the intent of corporations, there will be questions about the ultimate motive and whether companies are merely aiming to buy influence. Business is not universally seen as a trusted social partner and can thus expect major concern from government about engaging with business on sensitive public policy issues, as well as opposition from NGOs.

▶ The governance and accountability of business coalitions have not been explored in any great depth. To what extent do corporations take responsibility for the views and actions of such coalitions?

▶ The broader public policy legitimacy of single-issue pressure groups will always be suspect. The business sector may be well intentioned and acting in the broader public interest in demonstrating the need for additional public investment in education or housing, but does not face the competing social and political trade-offs in a resource-scarce environment as does the government.

Conclusion

The South African case exhibits some remarkable and progressive examples of collective corporate citizenship efforts, and demonstrates the significant contribution the private sector can make to a society in transition through dialogue, facilitation and institution building. By working collaboratively with government agencies and other stakeholders, business coalitions can play a vital role in facilitating a successful political transition process. Collective business responses have benefits such as the pooling of scarce financial and human resources and reaching scale and critical mass beyond the potential impact of any one corporation. This paper provides evidence of the private sector having contributed to the transformation process in unprecedented ways by promoting democracy and peace, as well as sustainable development in South Africa. The case is made that, under certain conditions, corporations can achieve more through a collective approach to improving state institutions and changing public policy than through individual projects.

A reflection on the lessons from the role of the business sector in the South African transition process confirms the imperative of business leadership, political leadership, relationship building and the need for responsive institutions. The findings validate the necessity for corporate citizenship thinking to extend beyond projects and even the value chain. There is an opportunity for the private sector to impact on public policy and achieve systems change in a way that will benefit the broader society and simultaneously improve the business environment. A better business environment in the form of good social, economic and physical infrastructure represents potential direct business benefits of the collective corporate citizenship approach. A better-educated workforce, less crime and violence, improved housing conditions and stronger social cohesion can also reduce the cost and risk of doing business and thus improve the competitiveness of corporations.

This study confirms that the private sector can indeed impact positively on the broader governance architecture of society and contribute to deeper systemic change. There is a need for a clearer conceptual understanding of the limits and potential for collective private engagement of the development challenges traditionally considered to be beyond its reach. Indeed, new thinking about the role for the private sector in global governance and systems change is essential in developing strategic responses to the complex sustainability questions facing the world in the 21st century.

Bibliography

BAC (2004) 'Business Against Crime', www.bac.co.za, accessed 15 June 2004.

Brink, D. (2000) 'This is a Matter of Trust', *Financial Mail*, 7 July 2000: 2.

Business Election Fund (1994) *Final Report: Business Stands for Building a Great Nation* (Johannesburg: Business Election Fund).

Business Trust (2004) www.btrust.org.za.

CBM (1997) *Submission to the Truth and Reconciliation Commission of South Africa* (Johannesburg: Consultative Business Movement).

CCF (2004) *Annual Report of the Colleges Collaboration Fund* (Johannesburg: National Business Initiative).

Coleman, C. (2004) 'NBI Note for the Record', informal briefing on the role of business during the SA transition, *SriLankaFirst/International Alert visit to South Africa*, 1–5 May 2004.

Corporate Citizenship Company (1999) 'What is Corporate Citizenship?', background paper for Commonwealth Business Council meeting, Durban, 13 November 1999.

Corporate Citizenship Unit (1998) 'Corporate Citizenship: The Main Ideas', www.wbs.warwick.ac.uk/bpccu/ideas.html, accessed 10 June 2001.

Eloff, T. (1999) 'The Role of Civil Society, Specifically Business, in Conflict Resolution, Constitution-Making and Transition in Divided Societies', paper delivered at the *Bellagio Conference*, Italy, 15–19 February 1999.

—— (2001) 'Partnerships between Business, Government and NGOs: Lessons from the NBI Experience', paper presented at the *World Bank Conference on Evaluation and Development*, Washington, DC, 23–24 July 2001.

—— (2004) 'NBI Note for the Record', informal briefing, *SriLankaFirst/International Alert visit to South Africa*, 1–5 May 2004.

Financial Mail (1994) 'How Business Helped', *Financial Mail*, 29 April: 20-21.

—— (2000a) 'Stealing a March on the Country's Criminals', *Financial Mail*, 7 July 2000: 10.

—— (2000b) 'Revamp to Spur Tourism', *Financial Mail*, 7 July 2000: 9-10.

Fourie, A. (2002) *Corporate Citizenship in a Globalising World: A Comparative Analysis of the Annual Reports of Ten Major South African Corporations* (MBA dissertation; Oxford, UK: Oxford Brookes University).

—— (2004) 'Peace is More than the Absence of Conflict: The Role of Business in Sustainable Development in South Africa', article submitted for publication in *People Building Peace II* (Utrecht, Netherlands: The European Centre for Conflict Prevention).

Friedman, S. (ed.) (1994) *The Long Journey: South Africa's Quest for a Negotiated Settlement* (Johannesburg: Ravan Press).

—— and D. Atkinson (eds.) (1994) 'The Small Miracle: South Africa's Negotiated Settlement', *South African Review* 7 (Johannesburg: Ravan Press).

Hall, J. (2004) 'NBI Note for the Record', informal briefing on the SA peace process, *SriLankaFirst/International Alert visit to South Africa*, 1–5 May 2004.

Hofmeyr, M., and N. Chapman (1994) 'Business Statesman of the Year Award', address at *Harvard Business School Club of South Africa*, Johannesburg, 10 August 1994.

NBI (1995/1996) *Annual Report 1997* (Johannesburg: National Business Initiative).

—— (2000) *Annual Report 1999/2000* (Johannesburg: National Business Initiative).

—— (2003) *Annual Report 2002/2003* (Johannesburg: National Business Initiative).

Nelson, J. (1996) *Business as Partners in Development* (London: The Prince of Wales Business Leaders Forum).

Ramaphosa, C. (2004) 'NBI Note for the Record', informal briefing, *Sri Lanka First/International Alert visit to South Africa*, 1–5 May 2004.

Spicer, M. (2004) 'NBI Note for the Record', informal briefing, *Sri Lanka First/International Alert visit to South Africa*, 1–5 May 2004.

SustainAbility and UN Global Compact (2004) *Gearing Up: From Corporate Responsibility to Good Governance and Scalable Solutions* (London: SustainAbility; New York: United Nations Global Compact Office).

Whittaker, B. (1996) 'Enhancing the Public Contribution of Private Companies', background notes to a presentation at the *1996 World Bank Annual Meeting Programme of Seminars*, Washington, DC, 28 September 1996.

Corporate Citizens, Colonialists, Tourists or Activists?

Ethical Challenges Facing South African Corporations in Africa

Daniel Malan

KPMG Sustainability Services, South Africa

Since the country's first democratic elections in 1994, South African corporations have steadily increased their investments and operations in other parts of Africa. The South African economy is by far the dominant economy on the African continent, illustrated by the fact that, although the South African population constitutes only 5% of the African population, the country contributes 30% of the continent's combined GDP. Given this dominance, there are interesting similarities between global multinational corporations and their impact on the rest of the world, and South African corporations and their smaller-scale impact on the rest of Africa. The degree to which South African corporations in African host countries manage to balance their primary economic roles with their social involvement (e.g. through local corporate social responsibility programmes) and their political involvement (e.g. through using direct access to government ministers or even heads of state) has an impact on how they will be viewed by their hosts. A matrix is introduced to describe these roles as those of corporate citizens, colonialists, activists or tourists. Donaldson and Dunfee's concept of integrated social contracts theory (ISCT) is particularly suited to provide guidance on ethical issues in international business. Its application can assist South African corporations to engage all stakeholders in host countries in an ethical manner.

- Business ethics
- Corporate citizenship
- Economic colonialism
- Social contract theory
- Hyper norms
- Moral free space

Daniel Malan is an Associate Director of KPMG Sustainability Services (South Africa), responsible for ethics and integrity services and is a senior lecturer in ethics and governance at the University of Stellenbosch Business School. He holds a master's degree in philosophy and a master's degree in business administration, both from the University of Stellenbosch, South Africa

✉ KPMG Sustainability Services, PO Box 4609, Cape Town, 8000, South Africa

▯ daniel.malan@kpmg.co.za

⊕ www.kpmg.co.za

S INCE THE FIRST DEMOCRATIC ELECTIONS IN SOUTH AFRICA IN 1994, SOUTH African corporations have steadily increased their investments and operations in other parts of Africa. Currently, only six of the top 100 companies listed on the JSE (Johannesburg Securities Exchange) do not have a clear African focus. For example, Shoprite Checkers is the biggest food retailer on the continent with more than 70 shops in 14 countries, MTN is the leading mobile phone service provider in Nigeria, Rwanda, Uganda, Cameroon and Swaziland, and SABMiller, the second-largest beer brewer in the world, is the market leader in all 13 African countries where it has operations (Van der Walt 2004: S6).

Many South African corporations have encountered resistance in African host countries, quite often because of aggressive management styles or because of accusations that they put local enterprises out of business. On the other hand, there has been a fairly predictable stream of complaints from South African corporations about corruption in these host countries, and the implied conclusion (often not acknowledged) that they are 'forced' to lower their own ethical standards to stay in business (the classic 'When in Rome . . .' argument).

Four senior executives from four large South African companies were interviewed during June 2004 to gauge their perceptions about the relative ethical standards in different parts of the world: South Africa, the rest of Africa and Western Europe. One corporation is a local subsidiary of a global corporation, one is a local unlisted corporation, one is a local corporation with a primary listing offshore and one is a local listed corporation. Using a ten-point scale, where 1 indicates 'highly unethical' and 10 'highly ethical', the four representatives clearly positioned the rest of Africa as the most unethical, Western Europe as most ethical, with South Africa somewhere in between.[1] The detailed ratings are displayed in Figure 1.

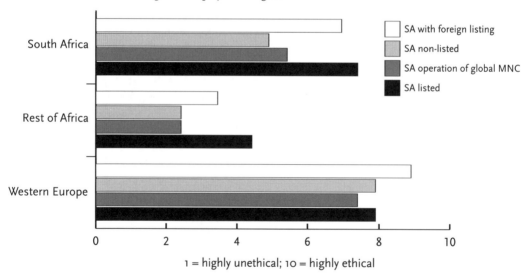

Figure 1 ETHICAL RATINGS BY SENIOR EXECUTIVES

---

1 It should be noted that, when asked to rate the rest of Africa, one corporation highlighted Botswana as a highly ethical country, on par with any western European country.

This paper attempts to move beyond the unproductive mode of mutual accusations of unethical behaviour towards an approach that will acknowledge differences in style and approach but—more importantly—accept certain core values that will provide a moral threshold for all contexts. This approach is based on the integrated social contracts theory (ISCT), developed by Tom Donaldson and Thomas Dunfee of Wharton University and presented in detail in their book, *Ties that Bind: A Social Contracts Approach to Business Ethics* (1999). ISCT is discussed in more detail later.

The South African economy in context

The South African economy is the dominant economy on the African continent, illustrated by the fact that, although the South African population constitutes only 5% of the African population, the country contributes 30% of the continent's combined GDP (gross domestic product) (Van der Walt 2004: S6). As was mentioned above, South African companies have steadily increased their investments in other parts of Africa. This trend is not restricted only to large multinational corporations. Box 1 lists the major South African investors in other parts of Africa (Thomas 2004: 37).

It is interesting to compare the similarities between the economic dominance of South Africa on the African continent and the global dominance of the United States of America. Figures 2 and 3 display the top ten economies in Africa and the top ten economies in the world in terms of GDP (2003 figures supplied by the World Bank; numbers in brackets indicate the country rating in terms of size[2]).

The dominance of the South African economy in sub-Saharan Africa is even more pronounced, with the country's GDP constituting almost 40% of the combined GDP of sub-Saharan Africa. However, the South African economy remains relatively small in global terms. The size of the world's number one economy is almost 70 times as large as that of South Africa, the 29th largest economy in the world. South Africa's GDP is in the same league as that of Hong Kong, Finland and Greece.[3] However, within the confined context of the African continent it is not surprising that South African corporations often receive the kind of attention usually reserved for American multinationals on the world stage. As can be expected, the large South African corporations often find themselves in positions where they have political clout.[4]

The position of South African companies in this regard is no different from the political power that other multinational corporations can exert, with the exception that, in Africa, South African corporations operate from a position of 'being part of Africa'. There is no doubt that this phrase is often abused, yet it is powerful, especially when some corporations also have ownership and management structures that are representative of South African demographics. However, even these companies often follow the traditional route where expatriates are largely white and male. One explanation that was offered for this phenomenon is that South African companies need all their black managers at home to meet employment equity targets!

With regards to South Africa's position in terms of foreign direct investment (FDI), Thomas (2004: 5) explains the contradictory, dualistic position of South Africa: it is competing as one of 53 African states to attract FDI to the continent, but at the same time is actively investing in other African countries, 'where their actions and the conditions

---

2 www.worldbank.org/data/databytopic/GDP.pdf
3 www.worldbank.org/data/databytopic/GDP.pdf
4 The political power of companies is often illustrated by comparing the size of global companies to the GDP of countries, and is not addressed in detail in this paper.

▶ Absa Bank	▶ Grinaker LTA	▶ Portcon (Transnet)*
▶ Airports Company of SA	▶ Group Five	▶ Protea Hotels
▶ ADS	▶ HSRC*	▶ Protekon (Transnet)*
▶ AECI	▶ Industrial Development	▶ Pretoria Portland Cement
▶ African Explosives Ltd	Corporation (IDC)*	▶ Profurn (JD Group)
▶ African Gem Resources	▶ Illovo Sugar	▶ Randgold Resources
▶ Africa Media	▶ Impala Platinum	▶ Rand Merchant Bank
▶ African Life	▶ Imperial Car Rental	(FNB)
▶ Alexander Forbes	▶ Investec	▶ Rand Water
▶ Altech	▶ Iscor	▶ South African Airways
▶ Anglo American	▶ JD	▶ SABMiller
▶ AngloGold	▶ JHI Real Estate	▶ Sappi
▶ AngloPlatinum	▶ JSE	▶ Sasani
▶ Anglovaal Mining (Avmin)	▶ Kumba Resources	▶ Sasol
▶ Aquarius Platinum	▶ Legacy Hotels and Resorts	▶ Shoprite Holdings
▶ Arivia.kom (Denel, Eskom,	▶ Liberty Bank	▶ Siemens
Transnet)*	▶ Lonmin	▶ Southern Mining
▶ AST (Vodacom)	▶ Massmark: Makro, Game,	Corporation
▶ Autopax (Translux, City-to-	Cash & Carry, Shield	▶ Southern Sun
City)*	▶ McCormack Developers	▶ Spoornet*
▶ Barloworld	▶ Mechem (Denel)*	▶ Stanbic Africa (Standard
▶ BHP Billiton	▶ Megasave (Shoprite)	Bank)
▶ BKS Global	▶ Metorex	▶ Stanlib
▶ Bosch	▶ Metro Cash & Carry	▶ Stauch Vorster
▶ Coca-Cola Sabco	(Metcash)	▶ Steers†
▶ Comazar (Spoornet)*	▶ MRI	▶ St Elmo's†
▶ Concor Construction	▶ MTN	▶ Sun International
▶ Council of Geoscience	▶ Multichoice	▶ Supreme Furnishers
▶ CSIR*	▶ Murray & Roberts	▶ Sybase
▶ Development Bank of	▶ Mustek	▶ Telkom*
Southern Africa*	▶ Mvelaphanda Holdings	▶ Tongaat-Hulett
▶ De Beers	▶ Nampak	▶ Transhex
▶ Debonair's Pizza†	▶ Nandos†	▶ Transnet*
▶ Denel*	▶ National Ports Authority*	▶ Transtel (IT)*
▶ Dimension Data	▶ Netcare	▶ Transwerk*
▶ Dunns	▶ Nedcor	▶ Truworths†
▶ Ellerines/FurnCity	▶ New African Capital	▶ TV Africa
▶ Energy Africa	▶ Nexsa (Nuclear Energy	▶ Umgeni Water
▶ Eskom Enterprises (incl.	Corporation of SA)	▶ Unitrans
EE-Telecom.)*	▶ Orbicom (MTN)	▶ V&A Waterfront
▶ Face Technologies (arivia)*	▶ Pep Stores (including	▶ Viamax*
▶ FNB (First Rand)	Ackermans)	▶ Vodacom
▶ Game	▶ PetroSA	▶ Woolworths†
▶ Goldfields	▶ Pick 'n' Pay (including	▶ Yale Security Group Africa
▶ Gray Advertising	Score)	
▶ Grinrod	▶ Plessey	

* Parastatal   † Franchise

Box 1 MAJOR SOUTH AFRICAN INVESTORS IN OTHER PARTS OF AFRICA

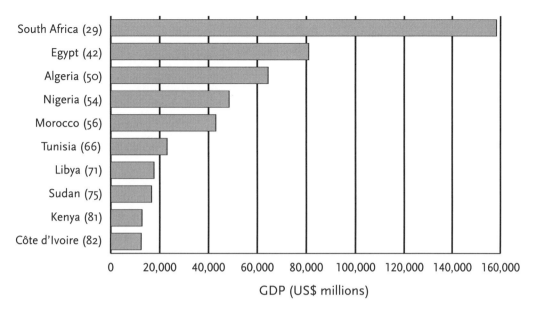

Figure 2 TOP TEN ECONOMIES IN AFRICA
Source: World Bank

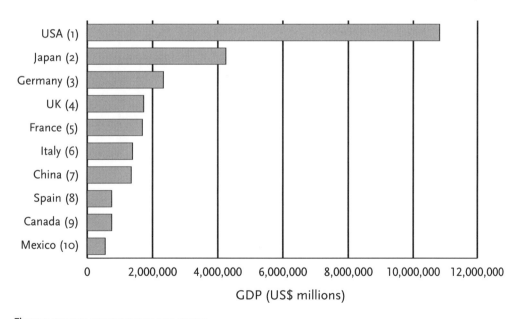

Figure 3 TOP TEN ECONOMIES IN THE WORLD
Source: World Bank

on which they enter frequently give rise to critical reactions from local interests in the receiving economies'.

Citizens, colonialists, tourists, activists

The degree to which South African corporations in host countries manage to balance their primary economic roles with their social involvement (e.g. through local corporate social responsibility programmes) and their political involvement (e.g. through using direct access to government ministers or even heads of state) has an impact on how they will be viewed by the different stakeholders in host countries. By plotting the degree of social responsibility displayed by corporations against the level of their political involvement in host countries, a matrix has been developed in terms of which corporations can be described as corporate citizens, colonialists, tourists or activists (Fig. 4).

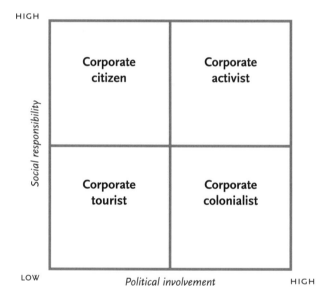

Figure 4 PLOTTING SOCIAL RESPONSIBILITY AGAINST POLITICAL INVOLVEMENT

Corporate citizens are viewed as responsible corporations that want to make a real and lasting contribution to the countries and communities within which they operate—sustainable corporations with a commitment to social responsibility as well as environmental integrity. Corporate citizens are defined by Michael Hopkins (1999) as companies that are 'concerned with treating the stakeholders of the firm ethically or in a socially responsible manner'. Hopkins further states 'the aim of social responsibility is to create higher and higher standards of living, while preserving the profitability of the corporation, for its stakeholders both within and outside the corporation'. Corporate citizens have high levels of social involvement, but stay away from involvement in the political process. Their intention is to profit from new markets, but they enter into such markets with a sense of humility and respect for local customs, traditions and even competitors.

Corporate colonialists follow strategies similar to the doctrine of economic colonialism: that is, acquiring 'colonies' or regions as a source of profit, without any real regard for the well-being of those regions. Economic colonialism is defined as an attempt 'to control another nation's economy. States can directly exert influence through economic policy and economic aid; however, economic colonialism may be most effective when applied indirectly through multinational corporations that invest in the key industries of targeted nations.'[5] Early examples of corporate colonialists were the charter companies, such as the British South Africa Company formed by Cecil John Rhodes, which was formed with the blessing of the British government. This company had its own army and police force—even its own flag and logo with the motto 'Justice, Commerce, Freedom'. A very crude indicator of the approach followed by corporate colonialists in Africa is the following quote from Rhodes:

> Africa awaits us still, and it is our duty to seize every opportunity of acquiring more territory and we should keep this one idea steadily before our eyes that more territory simply means more of the Anglo-Saxon race, more of the best, the most human, most honourable race the world possesses (Davidson 2003: 9).

Corporate tourists are companies that establish a quiet presence in host countries without much social or political involvement. This approach could be the result of a specific conservative strategy to ensure an easy exit if things go wrong or could be as a result of a lack of strategy altogether. Either way, the position resembles that of a tourist who is there to look around and stay a while, but can easily pack his or her bags at the slightest hint of trouble.

Corporate activists have the most problematic position on the grid. This is illustrated by the fact that the concept of an 'activist' evokes both positive and negative emotions, depending on the audience. Actively participating in both the social and political components of a host country seems problematic and the gut reaction is negative: the rule of thumb seems to be that corporations should become involved at the social level, but should refrain from playing a political role. Yet, to refrain from political interventions sometimes causes even more problems for corporations, as was experienced by Shell in Nigeria during the 1990s, when there was enormous pressure on the corporation to intervene in the political process to save the life of Ken Saro-Wiwa. This issue remains important even today, and, with reference to the Saro-Wiwa issue, the corporation maintains its policy position not to become involved in domestic politics, as opposed to making its views known on human rights matters. The following is an extract from Shell Nigeria's website[6] (my emphasis):

> In November 1995, leading Ogoni activist Ken Saro-Wiwa, MOSOP's leader, and eight others, were convicted and later executed on charges of incitement to murder. Some have said that SPDC [Shell Petroleum Development Corporation] did nothing to stop this. On the contrary, the facts are that, despite Ken Saro-Wiwa's criticisms of Shell in general and SPDC in particular, **we said that he had a right to freely hold and air his views**. During the trial, we consistently and **publicly stated that all the accused had a right to a fair legal process**. After the trial verdict was announced, Cor Herkstroter, the former chairman of Royal Dutch/Shell Group, also sent a personal letter **appealing to** the Nigerian Head of State to **show clemency on humanitarian grounds**. Regrettably, despite our appeal and those of others, the executions went ahead . . . **Like all Shell companies world wide**, SPDC **cannot interfere in domestic politics. But the company can, and does, make its views known publicly on human rights matters**.

An interesting example of a corporate activist is The Body Shop International. This activist role—albeit somewhat watered down currently—is neatly summarised by one

---

5   encyclopedia.thefreedictionary.com/Economic%20colonialism

6   www.shell.com/home/Framework?siteId=nigeria&FC2=/nigeria/html/iwgen/issues_dilemmas/ ogoni/ken/zzz_lhn.html&FC3=/nigeria/html/iwgen/issues_dilemmas/ogoni/ken/dir_kensaro_ 2703_0956.html

of the corporation's values:[7] 'We believe that it is the responsibility of every individual to actively support those who have human rights denied to them'. It is interesting to note how The Body Shop responded to the Saro-Wiwa crisis in Nigeria. The following paragraph is taken from the corporation's website:[8]

> [In 1993] The Body Shop began campaigning in support of Ken Saro-Wiwa and the Ogoni people of Nigeria, who were protesting against the economic exploitation and environmental destruction, caused by the Nigerian military dictatorship and multinational oil companies such as Shell. In 1995 when Ken Saro-Wiwa and eight other Ogoni activists were sentenced to hang, The Body Shop was at the forefront of international efforts to save their lives. This climaxed when The Body Shop organised for Ken's son to attend the Commonwealth Heads of Government meeting in New Zealand to press leaders to act. Following the barbaric execution of Ken Saro-Wiwa on November 10, 1995 The Body Shop redoubled efforts to bring about change in Nigeria.

One of the easiest—and seemingly most acceptable ways—in which large corporations become involved in the political process, is through contributions to political parties. In South Africa many corporations made contributions 'in support of democracy' to political parties before the 2004 elections. By way of example, SABMiller, the second-largest beer brewer in the world, donated R5 million to the six largest political parties in South Africa in its last financial year—this amount was distributed proportionately according to the support that these parties received in the 1999 elections.[9] In addition, a similar sum was spent on contributions to the campaigns and office-running costs of elected officials in the USA, and some donations were made in Central America for municipal and presidential elections in El Salvador. According to SABMiller's annual report, the donations were made to those supporting the beer industry in US states that permitted such donations.[10] The corporation defends its position by explaining that it should be 'active in protecting our legitimate business interests'. The general policy of the group is that it makes only exceptional political donations, in accordance with local laws. Other South African companies that made political donations during the last year included Anglo American, Standard Bank, AngloGold, Liberty Life, Kumba and Sanlam.[11]

When trying to assess the role of the corporate activist, it seems that there are certain occasions when it could be argued that there is a moral *obligation* on a corporation to become involved in the political process. It is not clear whether such a responsibility would arise only when there is evidence of a violation of a hyper norm (the moral threshold to be discussed in the next section). What is clear is that the current levels of involvement in the political process are far higher than the levels of disclosure about such involvement. Increased disclosure should be encouraged and will assist further research and debate on this topic.

Integrated social contracts theory

Regardless of their position on the grid, many corporations still get caught in unproductive mutual accusations of unethical behaviour. One way out of this conundrum is

---

7 More information available at www.thebodyshopinternational.com/web/tbsgl/values.jsp.
8 www.thebodyshopinternational.com/web/tbsgl/values_dhr_campaign.jsp
9 Report by Charlotte Mathews in *Business Day*, 29 July 2004.
10 www.sabmiller.com/SABMiller/Our+responsibility/Social+review
11 Companies such as SABMiller find themselves in the contradictory position that, because of their high levels of disclosure, they are often cited as examples when discussing controversial issues such as this. While the disclosure should be applauded, it is critical to deal with the issue itself and disclosure as two separate activities.

through the application of integrated social contracts theory (ISCT), developed by Tom Donaldson and Thomas Dunfee of Wharton University. This theory is particularly suited to provide guidance on ethical issues in international business (including social and political involvement of corporations), and in essence suggests the following:

▶ There is an absolute moral threshold (so-called hyper norms) that would apply anywhere in the world.

▶ Large corporations should have respect for local customs and traditions, without transgressing this moral threshold.

▶ Context matters when deciding between right and wrong. Although this might seem like a relativist escape clause, it highlights the fact that there are rarely easy ethical decisions to be made in the complex global marketplace. If applied in conjunction with respect for hyper norms and local customs, it does not lead to relativism.

ISCT has been described as a position that lies midway on the spectrum of moral belief, separating relativism from absolutism.[12] This approach assumes that there is something called 'moral free space', where stakeholders—for example, South African corporations and their host countries and communities—can negotiate micro social contracts that would determine what should be regarded as ethical and unethical. One of the consequences of 'moral free space' is that two conflicting conceptions of ethics can sometimes both be valid, depending on the situation. Therefore, if there is no absolute right or wrong (absolutism), yet relativism is avoided, what is the solution? ISCT combines two types of contract theory: micro contracts can be negotiated between or within specific groups or communities, while a universal macro contract ensures a level of consistency in the sense of providing the absolute moral threshold mentioned earlier. According to Donaldson and Dunfee, this approach holds fundamental truths to be relevant while allowing for legitimate differences within business communities and between historical theories. It also avoids the difficulty of the vagueness of macro contracts, while at the same time avoiding the problem that a micro contract can be morally out of bounds: for example, when a local community comes together and develops a contract that excludes members of a certain race or religion from that particular community.

Using the same thought experiment as the traditional social contract arguments of Locke, Rousseau, Hobbes and Rawls, the question that is posed by Donaldson and Dunfee focuses on how economic participants would define business ethics, instead of the classical question of what citizens would require of the government and how they would define political justice. The experiment assumes a group of imaginary contractors who are rational and knowledgeable. Departing from the classical social contract, Donaldson and Dunfee do not assume that these contractors are ignorant of all facts about themselves—they (the contractors) simply do not know in what economic communities they are members and they do not know their own level of personal wealth. It is also assumed that the contractors all have an underlying sense of right and wrong with which they were brought up. It is argued that these imaginary contractors will soon confront the fact that it is impossible to obtain consensus on a *single* morality as the framework for global economic ethics. The question then remains: how will they find a basis for agreement? Donaldson and Dunfee (1999: 28) argue that the following core assumptions will be accepted by all contractors:

12 Donaldson and Dunfee (1999: 23) describe the full spectrum as ranging from extreme relativism through cultural relativism, pluralism (ISCT), and modified universalism to extreme universalism (absolutism).

▶ All humans are constrained by bounded moral rationality; that is, humans are constrained by physical and psychological limits—they make mistakes, and existing ethical theories are not always sufficient to resolve difficult ethical dilemmas.

▶ Higher-quality and more efficient economic interactions are preferable to lower-quality and less efficient economic interactions.

▶ All things being equal, economic activity that is consistent with the cultural, philosophical or religious attitudes of economic actors is preferable to economic activity that is not.

Given these assumptions, Donaldson and Dunfee (1999: 46) argue that the hypothetical contractors will agree on the following macro social contract as the minimum terms for economic ethics:

▶ Local economic communities have moral free space in which they may generate ethical norms for their members through micro social contracts.

▶ Micro social contracts must be grounded in consent—individual members should have the right to exit: for example, a disgruntled employee who objects to a corporation's human rights policies in developing countries has the right to resign and find employment elsewhere.[13]

▶ In order to become obligatory (legitimate), micro social contracts must be compatible with hyper norms.

▶ In cases of conflicts among norms, priority must be established through the application of rules consistent with the spirit and letter of the macro social contract.

Hyper norms are defined as 'key limits on moral free space' (Donaldson and Dunfee 1999: 49), constituting principles so fundamental that they are discoverable in a 'convergence of religious, political and philosophical thought' (Donaldson and Dunfee 1999: 50). Different categories of hyper norms are identified: structural (e.g. the duty to develop and fulfil obligations in connection with social structures that are efficient in achieving social goods), procedural (e.g. rights of voice and exit) and substantive (e.g. promise keeping, respect for human dignity). Evidence in support of hyper norm status includes widespread consensus that a principle is universal, when the principle in question is a component of a well-known global industry standard or supported by major non-governmental organisations, known to be consistent with major religions or major philosophies and supported by the laws of many different countries (Donaldson and Dunfee 1999: 60). Using international bribery as an example, Donaldson and Dunfee (1999: 61) demonstrate the process of identifying hyper norms:

> A manager for an airplane manufacturer makes/is considering a payment of $5 million to go personally to the Minister of Defence of a developing country to 'win' a contract for jet fighters.

> It is not necessary to identify the full range of hyper norms applicable to all forms of bribery. The question instead is whether a hyper norm applies to this particularly egregious form of the practice. Transparency International, the OECD, the OAS, the Caux Principles, laws in numerous countries . . . leaders of major accounting firms . . . major religions . . . and major philosophies all support a presumption that this practice violates a hyper norm.

---

13 Given high levels of unemployment in both developed and developing countries, this right is clearly more complicated. Especially in developing countries, employees are quite often in a position where they have many dependants and no job security; it would therefore be extremely idealistic to expect them to resign from a job for moral reasons when they know they are unlikely to find alternative employment.

Finally, in applying ISCT to the ethical decision-making process, the following steps should be followed:

▶ Identify all the relevant stakeholders.

▶ Identify the relevant hyper norms (there is not a definitive list of hyper norms; the quest for such a list would resemble an absolutist approach).

▶ Determine that key norms are *authentic*; that is, there must be evidence that the norms are supported by a clear majority.

▶ Determine that the authentic norms are *legitimate*; that is, not in conflict with any hyper norm.

▶ Resolve conflicts if and when they arise through rules consistent with the spirit and letter of the macro social contract.

Guidelines for South African corporations

The decision-making process above seems rather abstract and theoretical. However, it is possible for South African corporations with continent-wide operations to apply this in a practical way. This should be done both individually (e.g. through changing existing ethical policies or developing new policies) and collectively (e.g. through the involvement of organised business structures such as chambers of commerce, trade associations, as well as government agencies that focus on trade and investment activities).

To kick-start the process it would require a few pioneering organisations to take the lead and open up the debate with the relevant stakeholders. It would be preferable for these pioneers to come from the private sector itself. However, this role could also be fulfilled by academic institutions or other non-governmental organisations. If this process can commence under the auspices of the New Partnership for Africa's Development[14] (Nepad) it would add to the credibility of its outcome.

Three critical requirements for success, based on the basic tenets of ISCT, are:

▶ Consensus on what the most important hyper norms are for the African continent.

▶ Increased knowledge about legitimate local customs and a change to a management style that would respect such customs. This can be accomplished through proper stakeholder engagement processes and by actively encouraging employees at all levels to challenge their own preconceived ideas.

▶ Development of moral sensitivity among all staff, moving away from rigid compliance-based ethics programmes to ones that would support the approach that context matters when making ethical decisions. This would require a radical shift in mind-set for many corporations and a move to a values-based approach, where trust—both internally and externally—will be critical for success.

---

14 The New Partnership for Africa's Development is a pledge by African leaders, based on a common vision and a firm and shared conviction, that they have a pressing duty to eradicate poverty and to place their countries, both individually and collectively, on a path of sustainable growth and development, and at the same time to participate actively in the world economy and body politic. Nepad is anchored on the determination of Africans to extricate themselves and the continent from the malaise of under-development and exclusion in a globalising world. For more information, see www.nepad. org.

A typical process for a corporation that would like to implement this approach would be to:

▶ Take a measurement of the existing norms within the organisation, as well as of the norms and customs that prevail within a particular country or range of countries.

▶ Codify these norms in a code of ethics or a code of conduct (or review any existing document). This document has to reflect the agreed hyper norms and should provide detailed guidance on the ethical behaviour expected of employees.

▶ Implement the code through an effective training and communication campaign aimed at developing moral sensitivity and decision-making skills, rather than simply a working knowledge of what is and is not allowed within the organisation.

▶ Provide ongoing support through the establishment of an ethical infrastructure (e.g. an ethics custodian and an ethics helpline) as well as ongoing stakeholder engagement.

It is unlikely that the majority of corporations with African operations will embrace this approach in the short term. Rather, there is a need for a number of successful case studies and a clear demonstration of the benefits associated with this approach, for both corporations and their hosts. Hopefully successful corporations will serve as role models for others, and ensure long-term, sustainable changes in the behaviour and attitudes of others.

References

Davidson, A. (2003) *Cecil Rhodes and His Time* (Pretoria: Protea Book House).

Donaldson, T., and T. Dunfee (1999) *Ties that Bind: A Social Contracts Approach to Business Ethics* (Boston, MA: Harvard Business School Press).

Hopkins, M. (1999) *A Planetary Bargain and the Bottom Line: Corporate Citizenship, Financial Performance and Staying Power* (Geneva: ILO, Enterprise Forum).

Thomas, W. (2004) *South Africa's FDI in Africa: Catalytic Kingpin in the Nepad Process?* (unpublished)

Van der Walt, S. (2004) 'SA maatskappye is leiers in Afrika', *Sake Burger*, 15 June 2004: S6.

Local Governance as a Complex System*

Lessons from Mining in South Africa, Mali and Zambia

Ralph Hamann and Paul Kapelus
African Institute of Corporate Citizenship, South Africa

Dan Sonnenberg
Sustainability Research and Intelligence, South Africa

Andrew Mackenzie and Paul Hollesen
AngloGold Ashanti, South Africa

Based on case studies of mining in diverse African contexts, this paper argues that implementing corporate citizenship at the local level may require support for more sustainable patterns of local governance, based on proactive and creative approaches to enhancing collaboration and responding to complexity. In some instances, weak and inefficient local government organisations, conflict between elected, state-centric government and traditional authorities, historical distrust or resentment of mining companies, and rapidly expanding expectations tied to local political agendas coalesce to contribute to vicious cycles of interaction characterised by low collaboration potential and high levels of unpredictability. Especially in such circumstances, traditional corporate citizenship activities based on unilateral company actions and stakeholder engagement are unlikely to meet their objectives. Rather, case study companies have learned that a more proactive involvement in moving local governance towards accountability and inclusiveness is necessary.

- Local governance
- Collaboration potential
- Complex systems
- Mining
- South Africa
- Mali
- Zambia

* Parts of this paper are based on Ralph's PhD, which was supervised by Tim O'Riordan, David Fig and Simon Gerrard, and funded by the Ernest Oppenheimer Memorial Trust and the Harry Crossley Foundation. Ralph is also grateful to Malcolm McIntosh for discussions on complexity theory held in August 2004 at the Sustainability Institute in Stellenbosch, South Africa. The paper has benefited from helpful comments made by two anonymous referees.

Ralph Hamann is Research Manager at the African Institute of Corporate Citizenship. He also works for the Centre for Corporate Citizenship at the University of South Africa, contributes to an international research project based at Harvard's Kennedy School of Government, and is visiting lecturer at Stellenbosch University.

African Institute of Corporate Citizenship, PO Box 37357, Birnam Park 2015, South Africa

ralph@aiccafrica.org

www.aiccafrica.org

Dan Sonnenberg is a co-founder of Sustainability Research & Intelligence, a research organisation mandated to supply the financial services sector with research and analysis of non-financial risks and challenges faced by business in southern Africa. He has spent the last ten years working on sustainable development issues, including work for Anglo American plc in a number of African countries.

Sustainability Research and Intelligence, PO Box 62419, Marshalltown 2107, South Africa

dan@sr-i.za.com

www.sr-i.za.com

Andrew Mackenzie is currently Manager, Corporate Environmental Affairs at AngloGold Ashanti. From 1998 to 2000, he was Environmental Manager at AngloGold's Sadiola Hill Gold Mine, where he was responsible for the environmental management system, working closely with his Malian colleagues on village relocation and community development matters.

AngloGold Ashanti, PO Box 62117, Marshalltown 2107, South Africa

AMackenzie@ AngloGoldAshanti.com

www.AngloGoldAshanti.com

Paul Kapelus is a founding Director of the African Institute of Corporate Citizenship and is currently its CEO. He has worked in the field of CSR in Africa for the past 13 years as a researcher, consultant, facilitator and as an employee on a platinum mine. Paul is also a member of the Global Reporting Initiative Stakeholder Council and the AccountAbility (AA1000) Council.

African Institute of Corporate Citizenship, PO Box 37357, Birnam Park 2015, South Africa

paul@aiccafrica.org

www.aiccafrica.org

Paul Hollesen is Manager: Social Development at AngloGold Ashanti. He has been responsible for developing and implementing the company's social policy. He has worked in the area of corporate social responsibility for the last ten years, first for Anglo American and De Beers and now AngloGold Ashanti.

AngloGold Ashanti, PO Box 62117, Marshalltown 2107, South Africa

PHollesen@AngloGoldAshanti.com

www.AngloGoldAshanti.com

O NE OF THE CHARACTERISTICS OF THE CORPORATE CITIZENSHIP DEBATE IS THE tension between, on the one hand, global standards and 'best practices' and, on the other, the implementation of such principles at the national or local level, especially in developing countries (Fox 2004). In this context, the proof of companies' corporate citizenship commitments is to be found primarily at the local level, where employees and neighbours are directly affected by corporate activity, and this is especially the case for such high-impact activities as mining (MMSD 2002).

Companies' international policies on corporate citizenship or sustainable development in many instances offer only limited support to companies' operational management at the local level. The implementation of such policies is often circumscribed or even impeded by social, economic or political processes at the local or national level, which are beyond the control of corporate managers. A common concern is that local circumstances create such complex and dynamic conditions that policy implementation is less a matter of rational action and more a matter of 'hit and miss' or 'chaos management' (interviewee comments).

This paper suggests that an expanded model of corporate citizenship may assist in its local implementation. Rather than see the company at the centre of a range of stakeholders, it ought to be considered part of an intricate and dynamic web of interrelated role-players involved in (un)sustainable development at the local level. This is referred to as the local governance system, characterised by varying degrees of collaboration potential and complexity. It is argued that corporate contributions to the emergence of more sustainable patterns of local governance require proactive and creative approaches to enhancing the collaboration potential and responding to complexity. This is illustrated by means of brief case studies of mining companies operating in diverse circumstances in South Africa, Mali and Zambia.

Corporate citizenship and local governance

Governance has been defined as the process of providing 'direction to society', whereby the emphasis is on the relationships between the state and other role-players, including business (Rhodes 1997; Moon 2002). Local governance hence refers not only to the role and functions of local government, but rather the manifold interactions between local government, local citizens and other groups. These interactions give rise to crucial aspects of (un)sustainable development, such as service delivery, infrastructure development and spatial planning. The emphasis on governance relationships, rather than just the role of government organisations, is also based on the prevalent policy incentive to increase citizen or stakeholder participation in decision-making and planning (UNCED 1992; World Bank 1996).

It is clear that corporations play an important role in these interactions between local government and local stakeholders, both in terms of core business practices and corporate citizenship initiatives. However, corporate management generally concentrates on the more immediate interactions between the company and its stakeholders, despite the fact that the broader local governance relationships have crucial implications for the motives and manifestations of corporate citizenship.

From stakeholder management to local governance

The predominant model of corporate citizenship emphasises the need for companies to engage their stakeholders (Waddock 2003). This model, schematically depicted in Figure 1, places the company at the centre of a range of 'persons or groups that have, or

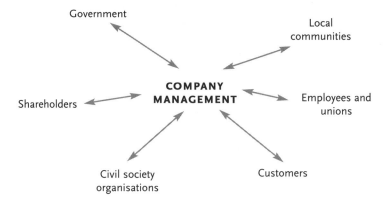

Figure 1 SCHEMATIC ILLUSTRATION OF THE STAKEHOLDER MODEL OF CORPORATE CITIZENSHIP

claim, ownership, rights, or interests in a corporation and its activities, past, present, or future' (Clarkson 1995: 106). The stakeholder model is also perpetuated by activities related to environmental or social impact assessments, particularly public participation (see, for instance, World Bank 1996).

However, it is apparent that the model in Figure 1 is a one-sided and simplistic representation of relationships between groups and individuals. For a start, insufficient attention is paid to relationships between stakeholders. Rather than existing in isolation of each other, local stakeholders, in particular, are embedded in a complex web of relationships. Furthermore, the stakeholder model places the company in the centre of these relationships—this potentially sidelines important processes that are outside the immediate ambit of the company, but which nevertheless play a crucial role in an effective corporate citizenship strategy. Finally, the stakeholder model often places insufficient emphasis on the role of power in the relationships between the company and its stakeholders, as well as between the various stakeholders (Banerjee 2001).

It is thus proposed that corporate citizenship be reconsidered in a way that sees the company as an inherent component of the local governance system, as illustrated in Figure 2. This system is characterised by the interests, roles and interrelations of various organisations and institutions (whereby the latter are defined broadly as the 'structures and activities that provide stability and meaning to social behaviour' [Scott 1995: 33]).

In Figure 2, the local governance system is tentatively indicated by the dashed oval. It encompasses the local development context, summarised here by reference to the sustainable livelihoods framework (Scoones 1998). This is important because local governance is determined by the development opportunities or challenges faced at the local level. The relationship between local groups will be influenced by the way individuals and groups relate to these development issues. The model in Figure 2 proposes four primary categories of groups or organisations at the local level that are commonly encountered in Africa (though there are likely to be others). These are local government, traditional institutions and authorities, other civil society groups, such as NGOs or community-based organisations, and the corporations present in the area. The organisational or institutional categories are also bound by dashed lines to indicate their self-referential or implicit definition. The arrows in Figure 2 between the context and the institutional categories indicate formal or informal interactions, such as communication pathways or resource transfers.

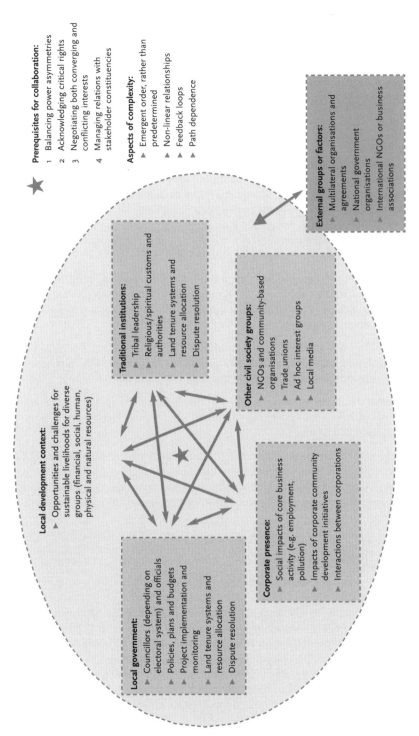

Arrows depict formal and informal interactions or relationships, characterised by the potential for collaboration and elements of complexity.

Figure 2 SCHEMATIC, GENERIC MODEL OF CORPORATE PRESENCE AS PART OF THE LOCAL GOVERNANCE SYSTEM IN AFRICA

Sources: see text

The potential for collaboration

It is apparent that the interactions between groups or organisations may be characterised in a number of different ways. In this simple model, we will emphasise those aspects that may contribute to, or detract from, the potential for collaboration at the local level. Covey and Brown (2001: 18) argue that 'the possibilities of productive engagement between civil society and business are greatly expanded as we learn more about how to manage not just cooperation *or* conflict, but cooperation *and* conflict in the same relationship'. They propose four conditions for effective collaboration between business and other groups:

1. **Balancing power asymmetries**. Despite the common concern regarding the misuse of corporations' power advantage, Covey and Brown (2001: 8) argue that 'the parties do not have to be equal in power—but they do have to recognise each other as capable of imposing significant costs or providing valuable benefits'. Nevertheless, the possibility for interest-based negotiation relies on the various parties having access to and making use of power-based strategies, including threats or actions related to legal recourse or peaceful protest (Lytle *et al.* 1999).

2. **Acknowledging critical rights**. Commonly accepted human, political and legal rights, as codified in international agreements and (hopefully) in national laws, provide the basis for establishing the 'ground rules' for interaction (see also Lytle *et al.* 1999; Boele *et al.* 2001).

3. **Negotiating both converging and conflicting interests**. All role-players need to develop an understanding of their own and others' underlying interests, in order to develop 'options for mutual gain' (Fisher and Ury 1981: 58-83).

4. **Managing relations with stakeholder constituencies**. Partnerships can only be formed fruitfully if the leadership of the different stakeholder groups is seen to be legitimate and accountable.

These criteria for collaboration emphasise that a company's efforts at partnership building may require significant preparatory 'groundwork' in order to establish the necessary conditions. This may include significant investments in supporting other groups to develop the necessary capacity or representation structures, or providing for facilitative or mediating activities.

Complexity and path-dependence

While Figure 2 may be closer to real life than Figure 1, it is still an overly simplistic representation. For a start, the organisational categories are not internally homogeneous or monolithic. The model needs to allow for conflict or discrepancies also within the categories. For instance, any corporate manager knows that corporate management is characterised also by conflict between individuals or departments within the organisation. There are also bound to be tensions between corporations present in a locality, over and above competitive pressures. Furthermore, especially at the local level, the important role of individuals needs to be emphasised. Charismatic individuals or interpersonal dynamics can determine local governance in a way that organisational policy cannot predict or influence.

Local governance is characterised by dynamic and unpredictable change. The straight lines in Figure 2 should not be interpreted to imply regular or predictable interactions. Rather, local governance and the role of corporate citizenship within it can be described fruitfully as a 'complex system' (e.g. Axelrod 1997; Dooley 1997; Portugali 2000; Rasch and Wolfe 2000):[1]

▶ The order of the system is emergent—that is, resulting from the changing pattern of relationships between elements—as opposed to predetermined.

▶ Relationships are non-linear. Simple cause and effect relationships are rare; instead, a stimulus may have a large effect or none at all, depending on contingent factors.

▶ Activities are linked through feedback loops, in which agents' activities are informed by the outcomes of their previous actions.

▶ The order of the system is path-dependent; that is, any future course of action is circumscribed by previous developments.

Hence local governance cannot be easily determined by decisive actions by any one group within the local system, including a corporation. The relationships implied in Figure 2 are path-dependent: the opportunities or constraints offered by the local governance system depend on what happened in the past. This history is not only manifest in the formal structures and relationships between institutions but also in the perceptions and levels of trust of the various local stakeholders. Proverbially speaking, it takes years for trust to be created, but only a moment for it to be destroyed.

Seeing local governance as a complex system has obvious implications for corporate citizenship. Rather than focus solely on the impacts of corporate activity or stakeholder relations, it brings to the fore the need for patient and sincere contributions to the emerging pattern of relationships between local individuals and groups.

Case 1: platinum and chrome mining in Rustenburg, South Africa[2]

The so-called Bushveld Complex stretches across the North West and Limpopo Provinces in the north of South Africa and contains the world's largest reserves of platinum group metals, as well as other resources, including chrome. The case study area is the mining region surrounding the town of Rustenburg in the North West Province, where platinum mining first commenced in the late 1920s. It includes the large mines of Anglo Platinum, Impala and Lonmin (respectively, the largest platinum companies in the world), as well as a mine owned by the Australian company Aquarius Platinum. In addition, the area includes the chrome mines of Samancor (a subsidiary of BHP Billiton) and Xstrata.

The Rustenburg area is confronted with severe sustainable development challenges. The mining activity in the area has led to significant immigration of employment seekers. This influx, in conjunction with the demise of severe population control measures applied by the apartheid state, has led to the growth of large informal settlements or squatter camps. These settlements are especially prominent around the mines' single-sex hostels—large residential compounds traditionally used for migrant workers—and they present the area with its most pressing social and infrastructure challenges.

In Rustenburg, the local governance system is characterised by its inability to deal with the challenge of the growing informal settlements, based on a vicious cycle of irresponsibility and lack of collaboration between key players.

---

1 It should be noted that some of the literature on complex systems emphasises the application of quantitative and computational modelling to social processes. While the concept of complexity is considered helpful in this account, such methodological assumptions are not encouraged.

2 For a more thorough discussion of this case study, see Hamann 2004.

▶ There are fundamental disagreements regarding responsibility for the informal settlements. Local government has the statutory responsibility for infrastructure planning and development, but it has been constrained by limited capacity, resources and legitimacy (see below). Furthermore, there are widespread perceptions that the mines have primary responsibility for social problems around the mines, due to the historical system of migrant labour and the continued reliance on single-sex hostels, which are generally accepted to be key contributory factors in the growth of informal settlements and social malaise around the mines.

▶ Widespread concern regarding the social impacts of mining has not been allayed by significant investments into community development initiatives under the rubric of 'corporate social investment'. This is because these initiatives have not proactively targeted the root causes of social problems around the mines. As noted by one mining company employee: 'Businesses thought that they needed to pay what some people referred to as blood money, but it never needed to be part of the business processes.' Further, companies have been competing to portray themselves as generous philanthropists, thereby impeding the emergence of collaborative development approaches.

▶ A key concern in the study area has been the limited capacity and legitimacy of local government. This has been due to the relatively recent establishment of local government policies and organisations, in the wake of the transition to democracy in 1994. It has also been premised on the conflict between local government and the dominant tribal authority in the area, the Royal Bafokeng Administration. Such tensions are common also in other rural areas (Ntsebeza 2002), but they are especially significant considering the Bafokeng tribe's ownership of much of the land in the study area, linked to significant royalties from the mines. Indeed, it is said to be 'the richest tribe in Africa' (Manson and Mbenga 2003). The Bafokeng's ownership of much of the land in the area also impedes initiatives for providing urban development and services to the informal settlements.

The above points coalesce to create manifold tensions between mining companies and neighbouring communities, as well. To illustrate, Box 1 describes the conflict between the Impala mine and local villagers, which is related to the history of the area and the tensions between local government and tribal authorities.

The above points also illustrate how companies are currently faced with a complex and tension-prone local environment, brought about by historically limited interpretations of corporate citizenship and problematic business practices linked to apartheid, in conjunction with significant institutional upheaval in the wake of South Africa's democratic transition.

Significantly, there are signs that this vicious circle of irresponsibility and lack of collaboration may be reversed into a virtuous one, based on shared responsibility and improved collaboration structures. This has been premised on powerful new incentives for greater commitment to corporate citizenship, linked in particular to the state's black economic empowerment programme (Hamann 2004), as well as increasing conflict and crime in the informal settlements. Companies in the area have now realised that they can only deal with these challenges by assisting local government in fulfilling its statutory responsibility for co-ordinated development planning.

SITUATED ADJACENT TO IMPALA'S SHAFTS AND IN PROXIMITY TO IMPALA'S planned open-cast mine, the Luka community is currently presenting the company with significant challenges. Community representatives have staunchly opposed the proposed new mine on the grounds that the community has not benefited from the company's historical activities in the area and has not been adequately compensated for negative impacts, such as cracked houses and alleged degraded water supply. Much of the resentment is based on the belief that the company's historical communication with, and contributions to, the tribal authority have not benefited the community. Hence the company has recently made efforts to communicate directly with community representatives in the local government ward committee, including the construction of a small office building to facilitate community meetings and interaction with the company. However, thus far these efforts have been thwarted. On the one hand, the tribal authority has felt threatened by the company's engagement with the local council and has ordered construction work on the office to be stopped. On the other, more radical factions within the community have threatened to derail the negotiations. This illustrates the difficulties of establishing community representation structures, particularly given the historical context of long-term neglect by both the state and the companies.

Box 1 THE CONFLICT BETWEEN IMPALA AND THE LUKA COMMUNITY

Case 2: AngloGold Ashanti in Mali

AngloGold Ashanti manages two gold mines: Sadiola (commissioned in 1996) and Yatela (commissioned in 2001), in the remote, rural Kayes Region of western Mali. Over and above adverse environmental factors, the area is also under-developed as a result of local tribal allegiances, which are at odds with the central government. The significant investment associated with the gold mines has brought rapid and significant changes to a formerly rural community. Development of the mines brought expectations of jobs and significant public infrastructure upgrading (including tarring of the road to Kayes). This also brought about an influx of numerous work seekers from all over West Africa, which puts significant strain on local infrastructure and social relations. Sadiola Mine also required the relocation of two villages.

The local governance context presented significant challenges to the implementation of corporate citizenship principles, such as the World Bank's involuntary resettlement guidelines, for instance. In particular, traditional village leadership structures were being usurped by the imposition of central state institutions, motivated by the need for state-supported infrastructure and renewed state interest in the area in connection with mining royalties. Hence traditional decision-making systems, based on patriarchal structures with village elders reaching consensus decisions, were replaced by elected representation structures in accordance with the state's decentralisation policies. However, these new governance structures have been plagued by conflict with the traditional authorities, as well as limited capacity and resources. Tensions have also increased as a result of other modernisation processes, including greater freedom and influence for youth and women.

These tensions were aggravated by competition for influence and access to resources related to the new mines. The emerging new leadership has frequently used mine-related decision-making processes or corporate giving as an opportunity for 'grand-standing' in order to legitimise and cement its power. These dynamics have made the field of community relations increasingly complex for corporate managers. Good relations with the local village chiefs and government representatives are no longer adequate for ensuring harmonious relations.

The mines' promise of social infrastructure development has significant impacts on these local governance dynamics. Elected representatives enhance their standing by being seen to be 'fighting' for the good of their constituency. Initial expectations for corporate support for basic services such as water supply, health and education have expanded to issues such as electricity provision, road development, water reticulation and public transport. The relocation of villages has further increased these expectations and corresponding pressures by local representatives.

There is thus a vicious cycle of increasing community expectations, more vociferous demands made by community representatives vying for influence and legitimacy, increasing conflict between traditional and elected authorities, and increasing difficulties faced by the company in responding to community demands and conflicts. This has been compounded by the involvement of international NGOs, which further increases the stakes for corporate management. In order to reverse this vicious cycle, the company has initiated an Integrated Development Action Plan, the objectives of which are to determine the development priorities of the district and to define roles and responsibilities of all the actors. Like in the Rustenburg case, therefore, the mining company has realised that it needs to play a more proactive role in moving local governance towards accountability and efficiency, if its corporate citizenship objectives are to be attained.

Case 3: the Zambian Copperbelt

From the 1920s, the development of mining activity on the Zambian Copperbelt, in the north of the country, has had a fundamental impact on patterns of human activity and settlement (Ferguson 1990). The economic opportunities in mining led to many thousands of Zambians migrating to the mining towns, which were dependent on the private mining companies for services and governance. A few years after independence (1964), mining was nationalised and put under the management of the national parastatal Zambia Consolidated Copper Mines (ZCCM). ZCCM was responsible not only for mine management but also adopted the mining companies' responsibilities for service provision and basic governance in the Copperbelt. The communities surrounding the mines became totally dependent on ZCCM for bulk infrastructure, water and sanitation, medical facilities, education, sport and recreation.

In the mid-1990s, Zambia initiated a privatisation programme under guidance and assistance from the World Bank, and this included the privatisation of the mines on the Copperbelt. A previous owner of mines in the area, Anglo American, became the majority shareholder in the newly created company, Konkola Copper Mines (KCM) (listed in London under Zambian Consolidated Investments), with significant investment also from the International Finance Corporation (IFC). The privatisation involved significant downscaling of the labour force and increasing mechanisation, which has resulted in large-scale retrenchments. This has had an impact on the lives of thousands of families in both urban and rural environments, as well as on organisations involved in local government and service provision. These organisations, many of which were newly formed after the demise of ZCCM, have struggled to cope with their new duties.

In this context, KCM embarked on a prominent corporate citizenship programme. Together with national infrastructure support programmes, as well as World Bank and donor-funded projects, the company has been involved in capacity building for effective service delivery and in numerous other initiatives, including small business support. In accordance with the privatisation agreement reached with the state, KCM developed social and environmental management plans, which were meant to facilitate and represent the company's corporate citizenship commitment. The social management plans were developed using the principles of the sustainable livelihood approach (Scoones 1998), emphasising a multi-stakeholder approach to defining a development strategy for the Copperbelt communities.

However, though these corporate citizenship initiatives are commendable, they have not been able to provide for sustainable development in the area, primarily because they have not been commensurate with the area's difficult history and the complexity and significance of the challenges. For a start, KCM's corporate citizenship initiatives have been unable to ameliorate the socioeconomic impacts brought about by fundamental business decisions. This is particularly pertinent with respect to the initial retrenchments associated with privatisation and the eventual withdrawal of Anglo American and the IFC from KCM in 2002, motivated by low profit margins (though an implicit motivation is often assumed to be the significant socioeconomic responsibilities in the area).

The Copperbelt scenario also illustrates how corporate citizenship cannot rely on the company acting independently. The entire local population is dependent on mining, not only in terms of employment but also in terms of local governance. This is particularly worrisome considering the need to plan for mine closure. The local government structures that were established in connection with the privatisation programme have generally been unable to respond to these significant challenges, which include unwillingness among residents to pay for services that were free of charge previously. There is no clear statutory guidance, much less negotiated agreement, on the roles and responsibilities of the different actors, leading to confusion and dispersed and unco-ordinated decision-making. Though local government has statutory responsibilities for service provision and planning, this responsibility is in many instances still held *de facto* by the mining company, leading to further confusion and duplication.

Partnerships between the company and other groups, including local authorities, NGOs or donor agencies, have been recognised as crucial prerequisites in the area. But these attempts are fundamentally constrained by the scale of the challenges; the proportionate partnership model seems exceedingly difficult to establish in the Copperbelt. Perhaps the key lesson of the Copperbelt is the need to recognise the fundamental limitations to corporate citizenship and partnerships in the context of severe and complex local governance challenges.

Conclusions

The relationships between an area's development challenges and local role-players tend to be characterised by vicious or virtuous cycles of interaction. In some instances, weak and inefficient local government organisations, conflict between elected, state-centric government and traditional authorities, historical distrust or resentment of mining companies, and rapidly expanding expectations levied at mining companies in connection with local political agendas coalesce to contribute to vicious cycles of interaction. Such patterns are characterised by low collaboration potential and high levels of unpredictability. Especially in such circumstances, traditional corporate citizenship activities based on unilateral company actions and stakeholder engagement are unlikely to meet their objectives.

Indeed, the case studies show that mining companies have learned that a more pro-active involvement in moving local governance towards accountability and inclusiveness is often necessary. In the Rustenburg area, mining companies are providing targeted and subtle support to local government, so that it can fulfil its statutory role for participatory and integrated development planning. In Mali, local government is less likely to fulfil such functions at this stage, so the mining company is playing a more explicit leadership role in developing the so-called Integrated Development Action Plan.

In the Zambian Copperbelt, the case study company has also emphasised the need for collaborative approaches, particularly because mine management has held such far-reaching and unsustainable responsibilities for local governance in the past. However, the scale, severity and complexity of the challenge posed by establishing a new, effective local governance system in the area are so significant that the company seems unlikely to have sufficient capacity or influence to move from a vicious cycle to a virtuous one. In the language of complexity theory, the 'tipping point' may be out of reach. In terms of corporate strategy, it is probably better to explicitly consider and, if necessary, acknowledge this possibility, than to raise unachievable expectations.

A key outcome of seeing corporate citizenship in terms of local governance complexity, therefore, is that it dampens expectations of what can be achieved by unilateral corporate actions. Rather, proactive and creative approaches are often necessary to develop and foster local collaboration structures. Collaboration is an emergent, self-organising process whereby successive steps depend on prior agreements and commitments, and final outcomes cannot be predetermined. In other words, establishing collaboration structures requires much time, dedication, and creativity from the company. But it is probably the most efficient and sometimes the only way of implementing corporate citizenship principles at the local level.

References

Axelrod, R. (1997) *The Complexity of Cooperation: Agent-Based Models of Competition and Collaboration* (Princeton, NJ: Princeton University Press).

Banerjee, S.B. (2001) 'Corporate Citizenship and Indigenous Stakeholders: Exploring a New Dynamic of Organisational-Stakeholder Relationships', *Journal of Corporate Citizenship* 1 (Spring 2001): 39-55.

Boele, R., H. Fabig and D. Wheeler (2001) 'Shell, Nigeria and the Ogoni: A Study in Unsustainable Development. II. Corporate Social Responsibility and "Stakeholder Management" versus a Rights-Based Approach to Sustainable Development', *Sustainable Development* 9: 121-35.

Clarkson, M.B.E. (1995) 'A Stakeholder Framework for Analysing and Evaluating Corporate Social Performance', *Academy of Management Review* 20.1: 92-117.

Covey, J., and L.D. Brown (2001) *Critical Cooperation: An Alternative Form of Civil Society–Business Engagement* (Boston, MA: Institute for Development Research).

Dooley, K. (1997) 'A Complex Adaptive Systems Model of Organization Change', *Nonlinear Dynamics, Psychology, and Life Science* 1.1: 69-97.

Ferguson, J. (1990) 'Mobile Workers, Modernist Narratives: A Critique of the Historiography of Transition on the Zambian Copperbelt, Part One', *Journal of Southern African Studies* 16.3: 385-412.

Fisher, R., and W. Ury (1981) *Getting To Yes: Negotiating Agreement Without Giving In* (Boston, MA: Houghton Mifflin).

Fox, T. (2004) 'Corporate Social Responsibility and Development: In Quest of an Agenda', *Development* 47.3: 29-36.

Hamann, R. (2004) 'Corporate Social Responsibility, Partnerships, and Institutional Change: The Case of Mining Companies in South Africa', *Natural Resources Forum* 28.4: 278-90.

Lytle, A.L., J.M. Brett and D.L. Shapiro (1999) 'The Strategic Use of Interests, Rights, and Power to Resolve Disputes', *Negotiation Journal* 15.1: 31-51.

Manson, A., and B. Mbenga (2003) ' "The Richest Tribe in Africa": Platinum-Mining and the Bafokeng in South Africa's North West Province, 1965–1999', *Journal of Southern African Studies* 29.1: 25-47.

MMSD (Mining, Minerals, and Sustainable Development) (2002) *Breaking New Ground: The Report of the Mining, Minerals, and Sustainable Development Project, May 2002* (London: Earthscan Publications).

Moon, J. (2002) 'Business Social Responsibility and New Governance', *Government and Opposition* 37.3: 385-408.

Ntsebeza, L. (2000) 'Traditional Authorities, Local Government and Land Rights', in B. Cousins (ed.), *At the Crossroads: Land and Agrarian Reform in South Africa into the 21st Century* (Belville, South Africa: Programme for Land and Agrarian Studies, University of the Western Cape).

Portugali, J. (2000) *Self-Organization and the City* (New York: Springer).

Rasch, W., and C. Wolfe (2000) *Observing Complexity: Systems Thinking and Postmodernity* (Minneapolis, MN: University of Minnesota Press).

Rhodes, R.A.W. (1997) *Understanding Governance: Policy Networks, Governance, Reflexivity and Accountability* (Buckingham, UK: Open University Press).

Scoones, I. (1998) *Sustainable Rural Livelihoods: A Framework for Analysis* (IDS Working Paper No. 72; Brighton, UK: Institute of Development Studies).

Scott, W.R. (1995) *Institutions and Organizations* (Thousand Oaks, CA: Sage).

UNCED (United Nations Conference on Environment and Development) (1992) *Agenda 21* (New York: United Nations).

Waddock, S.A. (2003) 'Editorial', *Journal of Corporate Citizenship* 9 (Spring 2003): 3-7.

World Bank (1996) *The World Bank Participation Sourcebook* (Washington, DC: World Bank).

Questioning Assumptions— Changing Frameworks

Business for Social Responsibility 2005 Annual Conference

November 1–4, 2005
Omni Shoreham Hotel | Washington, DC

Keynote Speakers Include:

Kathleen M. Bader
Chairman, President and CEO
NatureWorks LLC

Jim Skinner
Vice Chairman and CEO
McDonald's Corporation

Explore the integration of Corporate Social Responsibility (CSR) through more than 30 instructive breakout sessions that interactively cover a range of issues:

- Communicating CSR
- Emerging Issues
- Environment
- General CSR
- Governance
- Human Rights
- Public Policy

Register now at www.bsr.org/conference
and save up to $525.

About BSR

Business for Social Responsibility helps its network of leadership companies, the global business community and other key CSR stakeholders achieve success in ways that respect ethical values, people, communities and the environment. For more information, visit www.bsr.org or call 415.984.3200.

Business for Social Responsibility

CSR in Electrification of Rural Africa

The Case of ABB in Tanzania

Niklas Egels
Göteborg University, Sweden

Multinational corporations (MNCs) are beginning to explore low-income markets in Africa in search of legitimacy and growth opportunities. This paper examines the CSR (corporate social responsibility) aspects of this trend by analysing: (a) how the *processes* of defining CSR develop when MNCs enter low-income markets in Africa; and (b) what the *outcomes* of these processes are in terms of local definitions of CSR. A framework for analysing these two research questions is developed by linking descriptive stakeholder theory to actor-network theory. Doing this contributes to stakeholder research by showing how firms actively shape their stakeholder environment, the similarities of firm–stakeholder interactions and the role of artefacts in firm–stakeholder interactions. The developed framework is illustrated in a study of an Asea Brown Boveri (ABB) rural electrification project in Tanzania.

- Rural electrification
- Low-income markets
- CSR
- Stakeholder theory
- Actor-network theory
- ANT
- Tanzania
- ABB

Niklas Egels is a PhD student at the School of Economics and Commercial Law at Göteborg University, Sweden. His areas of research are international business and corporate social responsibility, especially in relation to multinational corporations in developing countries.

✉ Centre for Business in Society, School of Economics and Commercial Law at Göteborg University, SE-412 96 Göteborg, Sweden

🖥 Niklas.Egels@handels.gu.se

🌐 www.handels.gu.se

MULTINATIONAL CORPORATIONS (MNCs) ARE BEGINNING TO EXPLORE LOW-income markets in Africa in search of legitimacy and new growth opportunities. MNCs have, of course, previously operated in Africa, but they have mainly aimed at either producing products for export or serving middle- or upper-class local markets. Notable examples of MNCs now exploring low-income African markets include Ericsson, Asea Brown Boveri (ABB), Tetra Pak and The Dow Chemical Company.

There has been little research into this trend in general (London and Hart 2004; Prahalad 2005) and into its CSR (corporate social responsibility) aspects in particular. Such CSR-focused research is essential, given the potential magnitude of the impacts of MNCs on African societies. There are two main ways to analyse these issues. First, we can analyse how MNCs perform with reference to previously suggested definitions of CSR (e.g. Carroll 1979, 1999). Second, we can start from the beginning and closely examine how an MNC's social responsibilities are in practice negotiated and defined when it enters a low-income market. The second approach is used here so as to be sensitive to the 'unique characteristics of the operational setting' (Rowley and Berman 2000: 407) and to recognise that definitions of CSR mainly developed in Europe and North America might miss some of the uniqueness of low-income African markets. Two research questions are used in analysing how local definitions of CSR are established: first, how do the *processes* of defining CSR develop when MNCs enter low-income markets in Africa, and, second, what are the *outcomes* of these processes in terms of local definitions of CSR?

In developing a framework for analysing these two questions, I make three theoretical contributions to descriptive stakeholder theory. The previous stakeholder literature provides little understanding of how firms help shape their stakeholder environment, the processes of firm–stakeholder interactions and the potentially influential role of artefacts (defined later) in firm–stakeholder interactions. I argue that a framework for analysing these factors is vital for understanding how a local definition of CSR is established. This paper presents such a theoretical framework by enriching descriptive stakeholder theory with reasoning from actor-network theory. The resulting framework is exemplified using a case study of the Swedish–Swiss multinational, ABB, and its rural electrification project, Access to Electricity, in Tanzania.

Theoretical framework

Descriptive stakeholder theory

Descriptive stakeholder theory describes the interaction between organisations and their stakeholders (Rowley 1997). Within this general theoretical approach researchers focus on both the firm's side (e.g. Hill and Jones 1992; Mitchell *et al.* 1997; Rowley 1997; Driscoll and Crombie 2001; Jawahar and McLaughlin 2001; Elms *et al.* 2002) and the stakeholder's side of the interaction (e.g. Hill and Jones 1992; Frooman 1999; Rowley and Berman 2000; Friedman and Miles 2002; Rowley and Moldoveanu 2003). Analysis of previous research into descriptive stakeholder theory reveals a deficiency in three areas vital for understanding how local definitions of CSR are established. First, it is rarely discussed how firms are *actively* involved in choosing and creating their stakeholder environment: an implicit assumption is that a firm's stakeholder environment is a given. Second, little emphasis is placed on the firm–stakeholder interaction processes. Focus is instead on the *results* of these processes. The argument is that certain conditions produce certain results: for example, that the degree of firm centrality in a network is associated with different types of firm strategy (Rowley 1997), or that the degree of firm–stakeholder dependency is associated with different types of stakeholder strategy (Frooman 1999). *How* these results are created, however, is not analysed in previous stakeholder literature. Third, the importance of artefacts in affecting firm–stakeholder relationships is virtually ignored.

To shed light on these three unexplored areas of descriptive stakeholder theory and to outline a framework for analysing how local definitions of CSR are established, I propose the use of actor-network theory. While agency theory (Hill and Jones 1992), resource dependency theory (Frooman 1999; Jawahar and McLaughlin 2001), institutional theory and social network theory (Rowley 1997) have all been used to enrich descriptive stakeholder theory, actor-network theory represents a so far untapped theoretical resource.

Actor-network theory

Actor-network theory (ANT) deals with the processes of establishing facts and definitions. More specifically, the theory analyses *how* the processes, controversies and negotiations leading to the formulation of a definition develop (Newton 2002). ANT emphasises that the establishment of definitions affects the values endorsed in the local context (Latour 1986). The definitions a firm helps to establish can thus be treated as the practical definition of CSR in a particular local context. Hence, this paper defines CSR empirically and locally, based on the interaction between the firm and its stakeholders. Such a definition is sensitive to the potentially unique conditions of low-income African markets.

The concept of **translation**, used in ANT research in describing the establishment of local definitions, comprises four stages (Callon 1986a, 1986b):

1. In the **problematisation** stage a focal actor formulates the definition of CSR that this actor wants to see adopted. The focal actor does this by proposing roles for many other actors, and by proposing links between these roles. The aim is to define these roles and links so that the focal actor becomes indispensable.

2. In the following **intressement** stage, the focal actor attempts via a series of processes to lock other actors into the defined roles. To achieve this intressement, the focal actor attempts to draw on multiple artefacts and other actors in order to persuade, seduce or force the actors to accept the problematisation.

3. The result of successful intressement is **enrolment**, meaning that the other actors accept their assigned roles. If not, the enrolment has failed and the focal actor returns to the problematisation stage.

4. The focal actor attempts to **mobilise** all the actors involved in the problematisation to play their assigned roles. If successful, the mobilisation stage completes the process of translation and a network of actors is formed around a certain definition of CSR.

This actor network is initially fragile, and is particularly susceptible to **mutiny** within its ranks. Enrolment of actors is often done by enrolling spokespersons for groups of actors. Mutiny occurs if these spokespersons cannot persuade the actors they supposedly represent to assume the roles defined in the problematisation stage. The end result of several successful translation processes is that a local definition of CSR is established, solidified and stabilised with agreement between key actors emerging.

A theoretical framework can now be derived for analysing the two research questions. First, ANT shows that the processes comprising translation can be used to study how the *processes* of defining CSR develop in the local context. Second, ANT shows that the full range of *outcomes* of these translation processes can be treated as the definition of CSR in the local context. The link to descriptive stakeholder theory and the firm–stakeholder relationship also emerges, with the processes of defining CSR taking place between the firm and its stakeholders. According to ANT, however, besides the firm and its stakeholders, artefacts also influence these processes. The argument is that artefacts incorporate values and structures that enforce certain definitions of CSR (Callon 1991). Therefore, if one artefact is replaced with another, this can be expected to influence which definition of CSR is enforced. The three main types of artefact are: technical devices and equipment, texts and animals (cf. Law 1986).[1] After the case study, I will return to how this framework fills the three gaps I identified in previous stakeholder research.

Methodology

Research based on ANT tends to use a qualitative methodology, collecting data mainly from interviews, observations and written sources (e.g. Callon 1986a, 1986b). This qualitative approach is in line with the methods suggested for analysing the emergence of definitions in local contexts (Weick 1996), and for analysing MNCs in low-income markets in developing countries (London and Hart 2004). Like previous ANT research, this paper builds on data collected from interviews, observation and written sources. Thirty-four interviews were held with representatives of ABB and its various business stakeholders (e.g. Ericsson and Tetra Pak), non-governmental stakeholders (e.g. UNDP, World Bank, WWF and unions), governmental stakeholders (e.g. Swedish and Tanzanian government agencies) and village stakeholders. Each representative involved in the studied project in Tanzania was interviewed two to five times for an average of one and a half hours per interview. Given the limited written sources available at the village level, data here were mainly collected by means of observations and interviews. In contrast, more written information was used at the international level.

ABB's 'Access to Electricity' project

Initiating 'Access to Electricity'

In 2002, ABB approached the WWF (World Wide Fund for Nature) in the hope of forming a partnership for rural electrification. ABB's idea was to direct some of the funds it had donated to an existing collaboration to a rural electrification project in Tanzania. The choice of rural sub-Saharan Africa was related to the low level of electrification in this region. Of the 1.6 billion people lacking access to electricity around the globe, 500 million live in sub-Saharan Africa, making it perhaps the region most in need of electricity (IEA 2002). Additionally, 80% of those without electricity in the region live in rural areas, and 92% of this rural population lack electricity (IEA 2002). WWF International embraced the idea and assumed the responsibility for identifying a suitable Tanzanian village for a pilot project. WWF Tanzania (WWF TZ) recommended the small, remote village of Ngarambe, located just outside the Selous Game Reserve (one of the

---

1 To simplify, I use 'artefacts' as synonymous with the ANT concept 'non-human actors'. This leads to the inclusion of animals in 'artefacts' and to a broader definition of the concept compared with its conventional use.

world's most important areas for elephant and rhino populations). WWF TZ had worked with Ngarambe since the mid-1990s to increase the villagers' involvement in wildlife conservation and to strengthen democratic institutions, increase transparency and decrease gender inequalities. After choosing Ngarambe as a pilot project site, ABB launched its 'Access to Electricity' project at the 2002 World Summit in Johannesburg. ABB presented the 'Access to Electricity' project as its attempt to build a long-term profitable rural electrification business and the Ngarambe project as its way to gain the necessary experiences for this.

A controversial power source

After choosing the village, ABB and WWF turned to the choice of power source. For various reasons, wind, water and grid extension were rather quickly ruled out as main power sources, leaving diesel and solar cells as options. While recognising that diesel was environmentally unsustainable, ABB TZ and WWF TZ suggested that it was the only viable alternative given the project's budget. ABB's international 'Access to Electricity' manager, and in particular, the project manager at WWF International, were dissatisfied with this solution. Eventually, ABB allowed WWF to make the final decision on power source.

The stakes increased as WWF International departments started internally criticising the potential use of diesel with reference to carbon dioxide (CO_2) emissions, claiming that such a project would damage WWF's credibility. The WWF project manager had in essence three choices: endorse diesel, abandon the project, or renegotiate the project budget in order to broaden the range of viable options. Knowing that ABB was in the aftermath of financial crisis, the WWF manager deemed a budget increase highly unlikely. He decided, after lengthy discussion with WWF TZ, to proceed with diesel rather than to terminate the project. However, he insisted on using the most environmentally friendly diesel engine on the market and on conducting a feasibility study in the second phase of the project concerning the use of wind power as backup. The ABB manager agreed to divert funds from the budget to accommodate these suggestions. The choice of diesel has since then been questioned by several stakeholders at the international level, some at the Tanzanian level and hardly any at the village level.

Disagreement about the desirability of electricity

At the international level, ABB's stakeholders seemed to view rural electrification as highly desirable. The UN Water, Energy, Health, Agriculture and Biodiversity Initiative (WEHAB), for example, identified provision of electricity as one of the five most prioritised areas for development. Similar statements are found in the World Energy Council's recent report on the future of African energy (WEC 2003) and in the International Energy Agency's reports (e.g. IEA 2002). The World Bank, in collaboration with international donor agencies, is also scaling up its rural electrification efforts. To this end, its Rural Electrification Funds (REFs) have been or are being created in, for example, Tanzania, Uganda and Senegal. These funds will centralise and co-ordinate most international funding activities and provide subsidies for part of the initial investment (but not the operational costs) for rural electrical systems.

In Ngarambe, however, the villagers were rather sceptical, some initially not wanting electricity in their houses. This seemed partly related to ignorance of the benefits of electricity, and partly to a mistrust of companies in general and, in this case, of ABB. Additionally, some villagers' beliefs strongly opposed the provision of electricity. This was particularly evident with the village's traditional medicine man, who has yet to allow any ABB employee to set foot in his house, let alone install electricity.

Distribution cables below ground

To reduce costs, ABB TZ initially envisioned installing the distribution cables between the generator and the houses above ground. WWF TZ, however, rejected this option on the grounds that elephants, often present in and around Ngarambe, might topple the poles and get electrocuted. ABB accepted this reasoning and decided to incur the additional cost of burying cables underground. ABB, WWF and the village government all agreed that the villagers should dig the trenches necessary for this.

Several weeks later when it came to digging the trenches, the villagers refused to do so without financial reimbursement. At this time the only project participants in the village were two ABB technicians assigned to install the distribution cables. These technicians basically had three alternatives: do nothing and delay the project, give the villagers whatever money they had, or contact WWF TZ and ABB TZ. The only way to contact WWF and ABB was via a radio in a WWF camp 8 km away. With no car in the village, the technicians started walking to this camp on a road surrounded by head-high vegetation in an area with fairly dense populations of lions, rhinos and elephants. Upon spotting some lions down the road, the technicians decided to turn back and instead unofficially give money to some villagers for digging trenches.

Training village technicians

Since the villagers would be taking over operation of the electrical system, ABB agreed to provide necessary technical training for two villagers. The village government initially selected two candidates they claimed were best skilled for the jobs. After two weeks of training, however, the ABB team was displeased with their performance. For example, there were complaints that one of the trainees, a devout Muslim, left without notice for prayers five times a day. The team felt that in an emergency the trainee would choose to go to the mosque over repairing the electricity system, potentially jeopardising the electricity system or other villagers.

After discussion with the village government, ABB received permission to train four additional villagers. When training these, it became evident that the two initially trained villagers had been selected for tribal and family reasons, rather than for technical competence. One of the new trainees (referred to as the 'handyman') performed especially well, and the ABB team wanted to promote him to head village technician. This, however, caused serious controversy among many villagers, since the handyman was not originally from the village, was Christian (while almost all other villagers were Muslim) and had not yet been granted permanent village residency. The ABB team argued that the handyman's technical know-how was essential for the long-term functioning of the system, and that it was in the interests of the villagers to appoint him. Additionally, the team argued that tribe, religion and personal connections ('know-who') should not be decisive in recruitment. Eventually the handyman was appointed head technician. He is now more respected, trusted and accepted in the village and has also been granted permanent residency.

The future of Ngarambe and 'Access to Electricity'

ABB adopted a business model in Ngarambe similar to that proposed by the Rural Electrification Funds (REFs); that is, the villagers themselves should finance the long-term operation and maintenance of the electrical system. This financing is probably the greatest challenge for the Ngarambe village. While diesel was an attractive power source due to its low initial investment, its operational costs are high. ABB and WWF, however, seem to be supporting the village both financially and technically to such an extent that

Ngarambe's electricity supply is likely to be secure. It is, however, unclear whether ABB has developed a business model in which villagers can financially support the system's operation and maintenance themselves. Finding such a business model is necessary now that ABB is attempting to obtain REF subsidies in order to transform its not-for-profit R&D project in Ngarambe to several large-scale commercial projects in Tanzania, Senegal and Uganda.

Establishing a local definition of CSR

How did the processes of defining CSR develop?

I have suggested above that the processes involved in defining CSR can all be regarded as developing similarly, even though the results of the processes differ widely. The case illustrates this well. In all the described situations ABB actively participated in proposing roles for the various actors (**problematisation**). For example, ABB proposed that WWF should help by identifying a suitable village and choosing a power source within the assigned budget and that villagers should want electricity, help digging trenches, and help selecting technician trainees. More indirectly, ABB also defined roles for other actors and artefacts: for example, lions were expected not to threaten ABB employees and elephants not to interfere with the electrical lines. Even though ABB tried to persuade the actors to accept its problematisations (**intressement**), some refused. For example, the traditional medicine man and WWF (concerning above-ground cables) defined their roles differently, sending ABB back to the problematisation stage. ABB then returned with revised roles: no electricity for the traditional medicine man and underground cables, and the persuasion of involved actors started once again. As expected, ABB employed artefacts in the form of texts and technical devices to increase the odds of successful persuasion. For example, ABB used the installed and working electricity system and written testimonies from satisfied villagers in its efforts to enrol the traditional medicine man. **Enrolment** and **mobilisation** eventually also occurred to the extent that a functional electricity system was put in place, but there were clear cases of **mutiny** along the way: for example, villagers refused to dig trenches without compensation and village technicians were selected based on who rather than what they knew.

Translation processes can be observed in all the analysed situations of how CSR was defined locally. However, what can be said of the instances when these processes were successful from ABB's perspective? Three main patterns are evident in the data. First, translation failed and mutiny occurred when ABB enrolled a 'spokesperson' that later was betrayed by the actors ABB believed them to represent: for example, when the village government was enrolled to represent the villagers concerning digging trenches. Second, translation failed when ABB mistakenly perceived that enrolment had occurred when in fact it had not: for example, when ABB believed that the two most technically skilled technicians had been selected. Third, the likelihood of successful translation increased when ABB increased the number of artefacts in the network incorporating their values: for example, the likelihood that villagers would accept ABB's chosen technicians increased when a diesel system was in place that villagers could see occasionally breaking down, needing repairs and being difficult to maintain. If solar cells, which are easier to install and maintain than a diesel engine, had instead been chosen, the villagers might not have accepted the replacement technicians, as the originally assigned technicians would have been seen as 'good enough'. I will expand these observations into implications for MNCs in the concluding section.

How was CSR defined?

With an understanding of how the *processes* of defining CSR developed, attention can shift to the *outcomes* of these processes. In other words, how was CSR defined when an MNC entered a low-income Tanzanian market? Table 1 summarises ABB's and its most influential stakeholders' positions in the case's key conflict situations. The table also outlines the final outcome of these conflicts and provides examples of which values were enforced and which were neglected because of how CSR was actually defined in the case.

As seen in the table, several interesting prioritisations were made in the case: for example, the prioritisation of protecting wildlife by burying cables over electrification of additional houses, of unofficial payments over encounters with lions, of know-how over 'know-*who*' in recruitment, of proceeding with the project over CO_2 emissions, of minimising generator CO_2 emissions over the electrification of additional houses, and the prioritisation of villagers capable of financing system operation over those who could not. The general pattern emerging in Table 1 is that the local definition of CSR ended up somewhere between what ABB attempted to enforce and what its stakeholders demanded. ABB was unable to force its hoped-for CSR definition on the village, nor did it simply adopt the definition proposed by the villagers and other stakeholders. Rather there was the joint formulation of a local definition of CSR through myriad translation processes.[2] From this it is evident that it does matter who the stakeholders participating in the translation processes are for the way in which CSR will be locally defined; that is, it matters how MNCs shape their stakeholder environments.

Filling the three gaps in descriptive stakeholder theory

After analysing how the process of establishing a definition of CSR develops and what its outcome is, it is possible to return to the question of how the developed theoretical framework fills in the three gaps I identified in previous descriptive stakeholder research. First, in terms of firms actively shaping their stakeholder environment, it is clear that it was no coincidence that WWF TZ and the Ngarambe villagers became important stakeholders of ABB. ABB actively chose to enrol WWF and to enter Tanzania, and through translation processes was active in determining who would become its stakeholders. Acknowledging this *active* MNC role is vital in gaining an understanding of how CSR is defined, since, as shown above, the local CSR definition greatly depends on what stakeholders are involved in the negotiation processes. Second, in terms of firm–stakeholder processes, the case shows that the translation processes reveal the *similarities* of firm–stakeholder interactions leading to the *different* results on which previous research has focused. Third, in terms of the importance of artefacts, the case findings show that, for example, the diesel engine and the lions threatening the ABB technicians influenced the outcome of the firm–stakeholder interactions. If it had been solar cells rather than a diesel engine or horses rather than lions, the outcome in terms of unofficial payments to villagers and the recruitment of village technicians might have been very different.

---

2 It is worth noting that ABB's hoped-for CSR definition in Ngarambe resembled the proposed CSR definition in ABB's international policies. However, the empirical data provide no clear explanation for this resemblance so it will not be further discussed in the paper.

Issue	ABB	International stakeholders	Tanzanian stakeholders	Village stakeholders	Outcome	Values enforced	Values neglected
Power source	Low initial investment, i.e. bias towards diesel	Renewable sources	Slight preference for renewable sources	Indifference between sources	Diesel and feasibility study of wind	Electricity provided	Carbon dioxide emissions and electrification of additional houses (due to additional cost of feasibility study)
Generation equipment	Unclear	Environmentally friendly (WWF)	Unclear	No extra equipment	Environmentally friendly	Carbon dioxide emissions	Electrification of additional houses
Provision of electricity	Highly desirable	Highly desirable	Highly desirable	Disagreement among villagers	Installed electrical system	Electricity provided	Traditional values of some villagers
Distribution cables	Above ground	Unclear	Below ground (WWF TZ)	Below ground	Below ground	Protection of wildlife	Electrification of additional houses
Digging trenches	No unofficial payments to villagers	No unofficial payments	No unofficial payments (WWF TZ)	Unofficial payments	Some unofficial payments	Traditional Ngarambe culture and security	Fairness
Village technicians	Know-how	Know-how	Know-how	'Know-who'	Know-how	Skills, fairness	Traditional Ngarambe culture based on tribal and family affiliation
Operation financing	No subsidies for operations	No subsidies for operations	No subsidies for operations	Subsidies for operations	No subsidies for operations	Prioritisation of wealthy villagers	Equal right to, and need of, electricity

Table 1 ABB'S AND ITS STAKEHOLDERS' POSITIONS

Lessons for the future

First, managers need to be careful when identifying spokespersons for local actors, since mutiny may easily occur if the spokespersons are not actually respected. Related to this, managers also need to develop sufficient understanding of the local culture to grasp whether an actor they are attempting to enrol is deceiving them. To overcome these difficulties, I propose that MNCs should partner with organisations having strong local presence. In practice, this would often mean partnering with non-governmental organisations when entering low-income African markets.

Second, managers need to find a way to align the conflicting international and local stakeholder demands. I propose that this is most effectively done by carefully choosing what local markets to enter and with whom to partner; that is, by carefully choosing one's stakeholders. For example, WWF's previous work with Ngarambe regarding building democratic institutions, gender equality and increased transparency made it easier for ABB to achieve a local definition of CSR acceptable to both international and local stakeholders. WWF had in a sense already done much of the alignment work for ABB. Finally, to ensure that the values that MNCs want to see implemented are indeed established, managers should introduce numerous supporting artefacts (that incorporate the aspired values), such as certain technical devices and corporate codes of conduct.

References

Callon, M. (1986a) 'Some Elements of a Sociology of Translation: Domestication of the Scallops and the Fishermen of St Brieuc Bay', in J. Law (ed.), *Power, Action and Belief* (London: Routledge & Kegan Paul): 196-233.

—— (1986b) 'The Sociology of an Actor-Network: The Case of the Electric Vehicle', in M. Callon, B. Latour and A. Rip (eds.), *Mapping the Dynamics of Science and Technology* (London: Macmillan): 19-34.

—— (1991) 'Techno-economic Networks and Irreversibility', in J. Law (ed.), *A Sociology of Monsters: Essays on Power, Technology and Domination* (London/New York: Routledge): 132-61.

Carroll, A.B. (1979) 'A Three-Dimensional Conceptual Model of Corporate Performance', *Academy of Management Review* 4.4: 497-505.

—— (1999) 'Corporate Social Responsibility: Evolution of a Definitional Construct', *Business and Society* 38.3: 268-95.

Driscoll, C., and A. Crombie (2001) 'Stakeholder Legitimacy Management and the Qualified Good Neighbor: The Case of Nova Nada and JDI', *Business and Society* 40.4: 442-71.

Elms, H., S. Berman and A.C. Wicks (2002) 'Ethics and Incentives: An Evaluation and Development of Stakeholder Theory in the Health Care Industry', *Business Ethics Quarterly* 12.4: 413-32.

Friedman, A., and S. Miles (2002) 'Developing Stakeholder Theory', *Journal of Management Studies* 39.1: 1-21.

Frooman, J. (1999) 'Stakeholder Influence Strategies', *Academy of Management Review* 24.2: 191-205.

Hill, C., and T.M. Jones (1992) 'Stakeholder-Agency Theory', *Journal of Management Studies* 29.2: 131-54.

IEA (International Energy Agency) (2002) *World Energy Outlook 2002* (Paris: OECD).

Jawahar, I., and G. McLaughlin (2001) 'Toward a Descriptive Stakeholder Theory: An Organizational Life Cycle Approach', *Academy of Management Review* 26.3: 397-414.

Latour, B. (1986) 'The Powers of Association', in J. Law (ed.), *Power, Action and Belief* (London: Routledge & Kegan Paul): 264-80.

Law, J. (1986) 'On the Methods of Long-Distance Control: Vessels, Navigation and the Portuguese Route to India', in J. Law (ed.), *Power, Action and Belief* (London: Routledge & Kegan Paul): 234-63.

London, T., and S.L. Hart (2004) 'Reinventing Strategies for Emerging Markets: Beyond the Transnational Model', *Journal of International Business Studies* 35.5: 350-70.

Mitchell, R., B. Agle and D. Wood (1997) 'Toward a Theory of Stakeholder Identification and Salience: Defining the Principle of Who and What Really Counts', *Academy of Management Review* 22.4: 853-86.

Newton, T.J. (2002) 'Creating the New Ecological Order? Elias and Actor-Network Theory', *Academy of Management Review* 27.4: 523-40.

Prahalad, C.K. (2005) *The Fortune of the Bottom of the Pyramid* (Upper Saddle River, NJ: Wharton School Publishing).

Rowley, T. (1997) 'Moving Beyond Dyadic Ties: A Network Theory of Stakeholder Influences', *Academy of Management Review* 22.4: 887-910.

—— and S. Berman (2000) 'A Brand New Brand of Corporate Social Performance', *Business and Society* 39.4: 397-418.

—— and M. Moldoveanu (2003) 'When Will Stakeholder Groups Act? An Interest- and Identity-Based Model of Stakeholder Group Mobilization', *Academy of Management Review* 28.2: 204-19.

WEC (World Energy Council) (2003) *The Future of African Energy* (London: First Magazine and World Energy Council).

Weick, K.E. (1996) 'Drop Your Tools: Allegory for Organizational Studies', *Administrative Science Quarterly* 41.2: 301-13.

THE PROFIT OF PEACE

CORPORATE RESPONSIBILITY IN CONFLICT REGIONS

KAROLIEN BAIS and MIJND HUIJSER

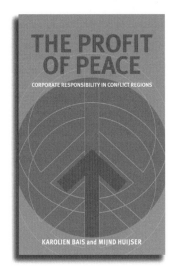

July 2005 / 144 pp paperback / 216 × 135 mm
ISBN 1 874719 90 X / £16.95 US$35.00

This book examines how multinationals can use their core business competencies to promote peace and stability in conflict regions and what role — if any — business has in diplomacy. To investigate these questions the authors interviewed CEOs and high-level managers of multinationals working in 'challenging' countries such as Afghanistan, Burma and Rwanda. The interviewees provided extraordinarily candid views on both the practical and ethical issues that occur when operating under extremely volatile circumstances. The lessons learned by these managers make the book invaluable for any manager working for a large company in a region of unrest.

The Profit of Peace is based on investigative journalism and contains many examples of best practices worldwide. It will be essential reading for practitioners, policy-makers and students involved with corporate social responsibility, peace studies, development studies and stakeholder management.

> ❝ Investing in conflict regions . . . requires perseverance and necessitates solving many ethical problems . . . Co-operation between the national government, tribal leaders, the UN, non-governmental organisations, embassies and multinational corporations is very important . . . This book, containing many examples of good efforts, is an important contribution to developing such a strategy. ❞
>
> *Major-General Patrick C. Cammaert, Military Adviser, Department of Peacekeeping Operations of the United Nations*

> ❝ Business cannot succeed if states fail. How business acts and uses its influence in conflict-prone situations can make a big difference, both for better and for worse. This book provides important insight for business executives and policy-makers. It will hopefully help to make business part of the solution. ❞
>
> *Georg Kell, Executive Director, Global Compact Office, United Nations, New York*

> ❝ To be able to engineer growth and productivity effectively, foreign companies need to know the social, cultural, economic and political aspirations of all parties involved in conflict. This book is a valuable contribution to the rare knowledge on this theme, founded on research that serves as an excellent reference in developing business strategy in conflict regions. ❞
>
> *Chandra Embuldeniya, President of the Business Council for Sustainable Development, Sri Lanka*

Greenleaf PUBLISHING

ORDER ONLINE AND SAVE 10%
More details at www.greenleaf-publishing.com/catalogue/profitp.htm

Orders should be sent to: Greenleaf Publishing, Aizlewood Business Centre, Aizlewood's Mill, Nursery Street, Sheffield S3 8GG, UK.   Tel: +44 114 282 3475   Fax: +44 114 282 3476
E-mail: sales@greenleaf-publishing.com   www.greenleaf-publishing.com

Seeking Common Ground

Multi-stakeholder Processes in Kenya's Cut Flower Industry

Catherine S. Dolan
Northeastern University, USA

Maggie Opondo
University of Nairobi, Kenya

In recent years, the Kenya cut flower industry has been criticised for poor labour practices, raising questions about the capacity of codes of conduct to improve working conditions. Multi-stakeholder processes are touted as one way to improve the effectiveness of codes, particularly where there is local 'ownership' and a broad range of stakeholders buy into the process. This paper explores the trajectory of ethical sourcing in Kenya's cut flower industry. It focuses specifically on the factors underlying the emergence of the Horticultural Ethical Business Initiative (HEBI), a multi-stakeholder body launched to guide social accountability in Kenya's cut flower industry. It identifies the points of consensus and conflict articulated by the different stakeholder categories within HEBI and the strengths and weaknesses of stakeholder partnerships for realising workers' rights.

- Kenya
- Codes of conduct
- Horticulture
- Ethical sourcing
- Multi-stakeholder initiatives
- Participatory social auditing

Catherine Dolan is an assistant professor in the Department of Sociology and Anthropology at Northeastern University. Her research interests are: the political economy of food and agriculture; gender and globalisation; ethical sourcing; and the social dimensions of commodity chains.

✉ Department of Sociology and Anthropology, Northeastern University, Boston MA 02115, USA

🖥 c.dolan@neu.edu

⊕ www.casdn.neu.edu/~socant

Maggie Opondo is a lecturer in the Department of Geography, University of Nairobi, Kenya. Her research interests are: smallholder agriculture; gender and labour rights in global supply chains; ethical trade and corporate social responsibility; trade policy and global environmental change.

✉ Department of Geography, University of Nairobi, PO Box 30197, Nairobi, Kenya

🖥 maggie@swiftkenya.com

T HE KENYA CUT FLOWER INDUSTRY IS CONSIDERED ONE OF GLOBALISATION'S success stories: a panacea for declining incomes that has brought thousands of new employment opportunities to the rural poor. Over the last few years, however, the industry has been the target of NGO campaigns and media exposés for poor labour practices. One way in which such conditions can be tackled is through codes of conduct that establish guidelines for responsible production, which gained prominence in the supply chains of African horticulture during the 1990s. Kenyan cut flower producers have been at the forefront in embracing codes, through both the development of their own industry codes and the adoption of overseas buyer codes. However, despite the positive steps that growers have taken to comply with codes, a number of employment problems persist. The fact that these conditions continue to surface in one of the most codified industries in the world raises questions about the capacity of conventional auditing procedures to detect workplace violations and breaches in codes of conduct.

Multi-stakeholder initiatives have emerged as one way to overcome the pitfalls associated with top-down conventional auditing, particularly where a broad range of stakeholders buy into a locally owned process. However, a key question regarding the legitimacy of multi-stakeholder initiatives concerns the nature of stakeholder participation in governance structures, including not only companies, NGOs and trade unions but also workers themselves. This paper, based on research in the African export horticulture industry, explores the trajectory of ethical sourcing in Kenya's cut flower industry. It focuses specifically on the factors underlying the emergence of the Horticultural Ethical Business Initiative (HEBI), a multi-stakeholder body launched in 2002 to guide social accountability in the industry. The paper identifies the points of consensus and conflict articulated by stakeholders within HEBI, illustrating how the cornerstones of multi-stakeholder initiatives—diversity and multivocality—shape the formation of genuine partnerships and the capacity to achieve workers' rights.

Multi-stakeholder approach

Stakeholder theory, which contends that firms have obligations to parties beyond shareholders, has been one of the most influential concepts in recent times, defining how companies should behave, whom they serve and the principles that guide their operations (Freeman 1984; Alkhafaji 1989; Hill and Jones 1992; Andriof and Waddock 2002). In recent years stakeholder theory has gained currency in international development circles where alliances between business, government and civil society are now viewed as a promising way to realise development goals of poverty alleviation and environmental improvement.

Approaches to ethical sourcing have adapted the principles of stakeholder dialogue to foster greater accountability in the business practices of global corporations. One example is the growing popularity of multi-stakeholder processes (MSPs), which aim to bring together a range of stakeholders to identify common solutions for social and environmental responsibility. By the end of the 1990s, these processes were rife in code initiatives as diverse stakeholders formed joint bodies to improve the effectiveness of code development, monitoring and verification (Blowfield 2003a). In Africa specifically, the creation of the Wine Industry Ethical Trade Association (WIETA) in South Africa and the Agricultural Ethics Assurance Association of Zimbabwe (AEAAZ), provided constructive models of locally owned, multi-stakeholder initiatives with positive achievements in workplace improvement.

Applying a multi-stakeholder framework to code implementation offers a useful way to build bridges between conventionally disparate interests and reduces the likelihood that business will 'act as judge and jury on social and environmental performance issues' (Blowfield 2003b: 311). However, several issues determine the extent to which MSPs can address the needs of workers. First, there is the question of local ownership. Research has shown that codes are most effective when there is flexible application and local ownership over the process of code implementation and verification (Tallontire *et al.* forthcoming). Yet local is not synonymous with the South. While several MSPs have emerged in the South,[1] they often operationalise a Northern agenda, with both the standards and the process of implementation derived from Northern models. Codes of conduct, for example, are founded on labour standards that privilege private property over community custodianship, the rights of individuals over communities, and secular, statutory legal systems over customary legal systems (Blowfield 2003a). Importantly, even codes developed in the South tend to exclude African (or otherwise 'local') perspectives from development and implementation (Dolan *et al.* 2003).

Second, one advantage of MSPs is that they move stakeholder relations away from conflict and confrontation towards collaboration and consensus (Blowfield 2003a). However, shared interests do not constitute a partnership. Stakeholders enter MSPs with different degrees of power, which determine what issues will be negotiated, whose interests count, and how the process is likely to unfold. Third, while MSPs are lauded as inclusive, they can also incorporate a narrow range of actors, who may not reflect the interests of intended beneficiaries (e.g. workers). Indeed, the question of how workers themselves are represented, particularly non-permanent workers, is often sidestepped. Thus, who participates in MSPs, and who has the authority to speak for those who are not represented, has a direct bearing on the likely outcome of such initiatives, and their capacity to ameliorate the conditions of workers in global industries. In the following sections, we explore these issues in relation to the Kenyan cut flower industry.

Methodology

This paper is based on Phase II of a research project on gender and social codes of conduct in the Kenya cut flower industry conducted in 2002. Phase I found that a plethora of codes were introduced in the sector but that the extent to which they addressed gender concerns was highly variable. The study also found that while codes can raise the standards of permanent workers, they generally overlook the conditions faced by workers in insecure forms of employment, which typically form the majority of the horticulture workforce. Phase II built on these findings by focusing on how the process of code implementation could be enhanced to improve employment conditions, specifically through participatory social auditing and multi-stakeholder processes. The research consisted of 100 semi-structured interviews and 13 in-depth focus group discussions (FGDs) conducted with workers employed in five Kenyan farms/packhouses that were applying codes of conduct. These were supplemented by in-depth interviews with management personnel on seven cut flower farms. Over 25 interviews were also conducted with government officials, trade associations, NGOs and union representatives.

---

1   In this paper, the term South(ern) refers to 'developing' countries, whereas the term North(ern) refers to 'developed' countries.

Codes in the Kenya cut flower industry

The Kenya cut flower industry is an economic success story. It has recently become the largest cut flower exporter to the European Union and currently employs an estimated 50,000 workers (Hennock 2002). The majority of export production is derived from approximately 60 medium- to large-scale flower operations (Mwarania 2004) that supply UK retailers and the Dutch Flower Auctions, both of which increasingly require compliance with social and environmental criteria.[2] By the mid-1990s, most leading Kenyan cut flower producers had applied codes of conduct in order to satisfy the requirements of their overseas customers. These codes, which are typically founded on ILO (International Labour Organisation) core conventions and the UN Declaration of Human Rights, aim to ensure minimum labour standards by establishing guidelines on a range of workplace-related issues. In Kenya, codes were introduced from four different origins: by dominant buyers such as supermarkets and importers; trade associations linked to the northern fresh produce industry; sectoral trade associations linked to the African horticulture sector; and independent bodies comprising business and civil society organisations (see Table 1) (Barrientos et al. 2001, 2003).[3]

Company codes	▶ UK supermarket codes ▶ UK importer codes
Northern sectoral codes	▶ EUREP GAP ▶ MPS
Southern sectoral codes	▶ KFC ▶ FPEAK
Independent codes	▶ ETI Base Code ▶ International Code of Conduct for Cut Flowers ▶ Max Havelaar Switzerland Criteria for Fairtrade Cut Flowers

Table 1 CODES IN THE KENYA CUT FLOWER INDUSTRY

However, the widespread adoption of codes did little to stem concerns about working conditions in the industry. By the late 1990s, a spate of media-generated reports described an industry riddled with employment insecurity, excessive overtime, sexual harassment, low wages and pesticide poisoning. These stories provided the impetus for the development of the Kenya Flower Council (KFC) and Fresh Produce Exporters Association of Kenya (FPEAK) codes. At the same time several high-profile campaigns against the exploitation of developing-country labour forced European retailers to rethink their stakeholder engagement, prompting several UK supermarkets to abandon their 'go it alone' approach and join the UK-based Ethical Trading Initiative (ETI).[4]

---

2 The continued use of methyl bromide raises significant environmental concerns. While efforts are under way to develop a suitable alternative through the Multilateral Fund of the Montreal Protocol, the industry has yet to identify a suitable and cost-effective alternative to enable a 20% reduction by 2005.

3 A number of prominent social standards have not been applied in Kenya's cut flower industry, including SA8000, ICFTU (International Confederation of Free Trade Unions) Basic Code of Labour Practice, and AA 1000. To a large extent, this stems from the market recognition of FLP (Flower Label Programme), Max Havelaar, MPS (Ethical Trading Initiative) Base Code among Dutch Auctions and European supermarkets.

4 Membership of ETI has grown to include 36 companies, 4 trade unions and 17 NGOs.

Yet it was not only UK retailers who were obliged to renegotiate stakeholder involvement. In Kenya, flower producers, who were in the firing line of allegations, were compelled to move beyond industry-centred solutions such as FPEAK and KFC, and come to the table with their conventional adversaries in a new multi-stakeholder steering committee, HEBI. As the following discussion highlights, HEBI has challenged the traditionally conflictual relationship between business, unions and NGOs through the shared aspiration of raising standards in the horticulture industry.

Origin of HEBI

The seeds of the HEBI process were sown in November 1999 when local civil society organisations mounted a successful campaign against workers' rights violations in Cirio Delmonte, one of Kenya's largest pineapple growers. The success of this campaign raised concerns in the flower industry, prompting stakeholders to develop the Kenya Standard on Social Accountability and a Voluntary Private Initiative (VPI) to oversee its implementation.

Yet the real impetus for HEBI came from the pressure exerted by transnational alliances of NGOs and consumer groups (Table 2). The Kenya Women Workers Organisation (KEWWO) was funded by the UK-based Women Working Worldwide (WWW) to gather evidence of code violations on flower farms in order to invoke the Alleged Code Violations Procedure of the ETI. KEWWO subsequently issued a public report cataloguing inimical conditions on flower farms (e.g. pesticide poisoning, sexual harassment and rape), and announced the launch of a campaign dubbed 'Produce Safely or Quit' (Lloyd 2002). At the same time, the Kenya Human Rights Commission (KHRC) issued a three-month ultimatum to flower producers to improve working conditions, failing which they would 'go international' in their campaign.

The gravity of such allegations prompted several corporate and NGO members of ETI to visit Kenyan flower producers in November 2002. In fear of losing their most significant market, rival Kenyan stakeholders came together for the first time to lay the groundwork for the formation of HEBI. Hence, in contrast to FPEAK, KFC and the VPI, which were locally initiated attempts to protect the image of the industry in overseas markets, HEBI was a product of direct northern involvement. While ETI and WWW only performed a facilitative role in the process, they were nonetheless pivotal to the establishment of a 'locally owned' MSP.

The objectives of HEBI

Following its registration as a legal entity in 2003, HEBI initiated a multi-stakeholder approach to code implementation and formed a tripartite Stakeholders Steering Committee (SSC) comprising members from civil society organisations and trade associations/employers,[5] four observers and government representatives as regulators. The SSC was given two broad terms of reference by the founding members of HEBI: first, to harmonise stakeholder interests and involvement, and to develop a participatory social audit system acceptable to all stakeholders including overseas buyers; and, second, to use the social audit system to assess the social conditions on flower farms and establish a baseline for future activities. The SSC embarked on this agenda by holding consultative

---

5 Unions were invited to participate as one of the tripartite stakeholders have yet declined to take part; there are still three (of twelve) seats designated for them.

Category	Stakeholder	Degree of engagement in HEBI		Seat on steering committee
		Instigator	Current	
UK				
Industry	UK retailers	High	Low	
Multi-stakeholder body	ETI	High	Medium	
NGOs	CAFOD, Christian Aid, Oxfam	Medium	Low	
	Women Working Worldwide	High	Medium	
Trade unions	IUF	Medium	Low	
International government agencies	ILO	Low	Low	
Kenya				
Trade unions	COTU	Low	None	✓ Declined
	KPAWU	Low	None	✓ Declined
Industry	FPEAK	Medium	High	
	KFC	Medium	High	
	Federation of Kenya Employers (FKE)	Low	Low	
	Agricultural Employers Association (AEA)	High	Low	
NGOs	Africa Now	Low	High	✓ Observer
	KHRC	High	High	
	KEWWO	High	High	
	Workers' Rights Alert (WRA)	High	High	
Government	Ministry of Agriculture	Low	Medium	✓ Facilitator
	Ministry of Labour	Low	Medium	
	Ministry of Trade and Industry	Low	Medium	
International government agencies	Royal Netherlands Embassy	Low	Medium	✓ Observer
	UK Department for International Development	Medium	Medium	✓ Observer
	United States Agency for International Development	Low	Medium	
Multi-stakeholder body	VPI	High	None	

Table 2 STAKEHOLDER ENGAGEMENT IN HEBI

meetings with relevant government entities and international stakeholders, and ultimately developing the HEBI draft code (Box 1). Once the code had been drafted, the SSC, in conjunction with an independent social auditor, developed a methodology for conducting participatory social audits and trained 23 local auditors.

1. Child labour
2. Forced labour
3. Health and safety
4. Freedom of association and right to collective bargaining
5. Discrimination
6. Disciplinary practices
7. Working hours
8. Compensation
9. Regular employment provided
10. Management systems
11. Protection of the environment

Box 1 HEBI BASE CODE

The HEBI code

The draft HEBI code draws most of its criteria from established African and international standards, resembling most closely the orientation of the ETI Base Code. Yet in contrast to ETI, the HEBI draft code is part of a wider movement to localise social codes in African horticulture. It therefore includes a number of criteria specific to the Kenya national context such as the inclusion of HIV/AIDS in health and safety training, term limits on informal forms of employment, and a number of gender-specific criteria (as identified by workers themselves) such as new provisions on maternity leave, sexual harassment and worker complaints.

One of the aspirations of MSPs is to achieve standardisation across codes. While the draft code includes new criteria, it nevertheless competes with a number of codes (see Table 1) that are currently adopted by flower producers. Should the HEBI code be finalised, it could replace prevailing social codes such as ETI and the ICC (International Code of Conduct for the Production of Cut Flowers). However, it is unlikely to replace KFC and MPS (Milieu Project Sierteelt), which contain technical and environmental criteria that are important for European markets. The widespread adoption of HEBI will therefore require negotiation with other standardisation bodies and strong recognition in the marketplace.

Yet the HEBI process is broader than the formal written code. Realising that even the most sensitive codes are meaningless if the sensitivity is not achieved in practice, HEBI has focused on developing a participatory social auditing (PSA) framework as a way to identify poor working conditions. Research has shown that PSA is more likely to build trust, promote dialogue and expose workplace issues that can remain hidden in a one-size-fits-all auditing approach. In 2003 HEBI applied PSA methods in eight pilot social audits (with a multi-stakeholder audit team) as part of a learning initiative to trial participatory methods in social auditing.

HEBI has the potential to develop into a credible social auditing institution; however, its long-term viability is increasingly questioned. Apart from the eight pilot audits, only one farm has undergone a formal audit of the HEBI code, which chose to engage an independent 'corporate' auditor. Yet the failure of HEBI to achieve early success stems from factors that underscore MSPs more broadly—the politics of stakeholder relations—an issue to which we now turn.

Participation in HEBI

The legitimacy of MSPs is generally conferred through the equitable representation of stakeholder views and the embodiment of democratic principles of accountability and transparency (Utting 2002). Yet while HEBI incorporated a range of actors from civil society, government and industry, the founding members were largely drawn from the membership of the defunct VPI process, contributing to the perception that it is an initiative driven by a select group of stakeholders. There was no attempt to include less visible actors such as small and medium-sized producers not represented by KFC or FPEAK, women's and other workers organisations with a stake in Kenyan horticulture, or workers themselves. In fact, workers are the most marginalised group of primary stakeholders within HEBI as it is assumed that their interests are adequately served by the civil society organisations representing them. Furthermore, HEBI is increasingly identified with the personalities of the individuals on the SSC rather than with the organisations they represent. Taken together these factors raise questions about the long-term viability of HEBI and the extent to which HEBI represents a broad-based, democratic initiative.

Conflict and partnership

As the above discussion highlights, the HEBI process has been marked by tension between stakeholder groups, stemming in part from the vested interests that preceded its establishment. However, conflict is not necessarily an obstacle to social equity. Indeed, it was the polarisation of stakeholder interests that initially generated the need for dialogue in the industry. However, even where conflict is empowering, power relations between stakeholders continue to shape the issues that are raised, the alliances that are formed and the successes that multi-stakeholder bodies such as HEBI are able to achieve.

Trade unions and NGOs

One criterion that affords legitimacy to MSPs is the involvement of trade unions in their governance structures.[6] Yet to date unions have refused to participate in HEBI. This reluctance stems from a number of factors related to Kenya's sociopolitical climate but is primarily a reflection of the problematic relationships between unions and NGOs, both of which purport to represent workers. For their part, NGOs question labour's claim to leadership given the fact that only a minority of flower workers (3,400) are members of

---

6 See the study conducted by the Ecologic Institute for International and European Environmental Policy for an analysis of the role of labour unions in initiatives for sustainable consumption and production (Heins 2004).

KPAWU (Kenya Plantation and Agricultural Workers' Union). NGOs argue that trade unions tailor their services to a minority of male permanent workers, excluding female informal workers, who form the majority of the labour force and are not protected by labour law.

On the other hand, trade unions contend that it is their obligation to protect workers' rights. Animosities between NGOs and trade unions have intensified since the intro-duction of private voluntary initiatives, which trade unions perceive as no substitute for strong laws, union organising and collective bargaining. The Central Organisation of Trade Unions (COTU), for example, claims that 'NGOs and human-rights activists have no locus standing in as far as the labour market problems in this country are concerned' (cited by *East African Standard* 2003). As companies bring in NGOs (under the auspices of HEBI) to train workers and staff on labour issues, there is the potential for the turf war between NGOs and trade unions to escalate. Yet such conflicts are not irreconcilable; the Germany-based Flower Label Programme (FLP) provides a model of stakeholder collaboration that has reconciled the vested interests of NGOs and unions in both North and South (Heins 2004).

Union–industry

The relationship between flower producers and trade unions soured considerably in 1999 when the General Secretary of KPAWU castigated Oserian, one of Kenya's largest flower farms for their 'perpetual enslaving of workers . . . tantamount to both human and trade union rights abuse' (Atwoli cited by Fian 2004). However, the KFC, who worked with KPAWU and COTU in the development of the KFC code, has eased these hostilities. The introduction of social codes has also spawned greater openness to union repre-sentation due to the provisions on freedom of association and the right to collective bargaining.

Industry–NGOs

Prior to the establishment of HEBI relations between the flower growers and civil society organisations were openly hostile. A monitor for KHRC, for example, described the industry to media representatives as 'total exploitation' (cited by Green 2002). However, there are signs that the antagonism is abating with both parties acknowledging a need to maintain dialogue, if only to serve their own interest. Companies view such dialogue as a way to thwart scandals emanating from NGOs, while the latter perceive improved business–NGO relations as a stepping stone towards better workplace practices (Bendell and Murphy 1999: 3).

Industry–government

The Kenya flower industry has benefited from very little government interference. How-ever, in recent years, the success of the industry has sparked the interest of government officials who wish to gain control of a lucrative revenue stream. These efforts have met with strong resistance from horticultural associations such as FPEAK and KFC, who argue that increased state regulation over the industry will create inefficiencies and undermine the industry's profitability. HEBI, too, has supported this position and called for the government to maintain a facilitative rather than regulatory role (Mwai 2004). As a result, the government has reluctantly agreed to assist the efforts of HEBI.

Reconciliation and consensus

While there are serious challenges to reconciling divergent stakeholder interests, there is nevertheless a consensus that a multi-stakeholder approach to code implementation may be the only way to resolve some of the persistent employment problems facing workers in the industry, while maintaining Kenya's reputation in European markets. Towards this end, stakeholders within HEBI have adopted three main processes:

▶ **Confidentiality agreement**. The signing of the confidentiality agreement by all the SSC members and observers has been instrumental in reducing tensions among the different stakeholders. The confidentiality agreement prohibits members (in their individual capacity) from releasing information (e.g. audit results) to the public, particularly to the media. This measure is critical to an industry that has been stung by adverse publicity and NGO campaigns.

▶ **Observers**. The mediating role played by the observers has helped HEBI to achieve a level of cohesion that was hitherto unimaginable. The observers have been responsible for funding training programmes and meetings, and providing the initial funds for the establishment of the HEBI secretariat. This has culminated in delegating the management of HEBI to an independent secretariat, with the appointment of an administrator in 2004. It is anticipated that the secretariat will oversee the finalisation of the draft Base Code and establish HEBI as the regulating body for the Kenya horticultural industry.

▶ **Pre-audits**. The involvement of stakeholders in the social audit process, including civil society, has been important in building confidence and increasing the acceptance of the audit findings among flower producers. By the time the audits were completed on the eight sample flower farms, a rapport between civil society and the flower producers had been established. The audits also served to increase awareness of the benefits of social codes among participating stakeholders.

Conclusion

Multi-stakeholder processes can represent an advance on codes that are unilaterally designed and implemented, engendering benefits for workers and the wider business community. Such initiatives also assume increasing importance in countries such as Kenya, where years of fiscal crisis have weakened the state's ability to enforce labour and environmental laws. Yet, as noted, who participates in the governance structures of multi-stakeholder processes and how they participate influences the long-term prospects of such initiatives and their likely beneficiaries.

While pressures for social justice in the flower industry have brought conventional adversaries together, HEBI faces several challenges to translating these efforts into a sustainable initiative. These challenges relate to the legitimacy awarded to PSA in Northern markets as well as the nature of stakeholder relations in global supply chains. First, PSA is an important component of the HEBI process. While measuring code compliance through social auditing has garnered considerable attention in corporate responsibility circles, the question of who audits and what type of social auditing is legitimised raises issues for organisations such as HEBI. The methods of corporate social auditors (e.g. KPMG, SGS, BVQI), for example, have been criticised for bypassing the concerns of marginalised workers and failing to capture sensitive issues such as gender discrimination and sexual harassment (Barrientos *et al.* 2003). However, such certification systems continue to be valued by Northern buyers (despite their costs) as they provide consistency in auditing systems across a range of industries and countries (Courville 2003).[7] While HEBI auditors are well equipped to identify deep-seated workplace problems (through their knowledge of language, local culture, and their capacity to perform regular monitoring), they will be unable to expand their institutional role if corporate auditors remain privileged in the marketplace.

Second, HEBI seeks to foster a democratic multi-stakeholder process that can accommodate competing interests. However, this model assumes that stakeholders are situated on a level playing field and that power asymmetries diminish within multi-stakeholder bodies. While HEBI has cultivated a space for stakeholder engagement, the realisation of genuine partnerships necessitates a degree of trust and power sharing that is uncharacteristic in global supply chains. In fact, the power to determine which stakeholders are called to the bargaining table and whose voices are validated is significantly influenced by market pressures beyond Kenya. The fact that HEBI continues to receive international support despite the absence of trade union participation is indicative of how Northern actors continue to shape the trajectory of MSPs. Further, apart from the trade unions, the most marginalised stakeholders in HEBI are workers whose conditions such initiatives seek to improve. Yet the integrity of MSPs necessitates that *all* stakeholders are included in the process. Ultimately, it is only through a process of genuine inclusion, which accommodates dissent and makes explicit power inequalities, that the long-term sustainability of HEBI can be realised.

References

Alkhafaji, A.F. (1989) *A Stakeholder Approach to Corporate Governance: Managing in a Dynamic Environment* (New York: Quorum Books).

Andriof, J., and S. Waddock (2002) 'Unfolding Stakeholder Engagement', in *Unfolding Stakeholder Thinking: Theory, Responsibility and Engagement* (Sheffield, UK: Greenleaf publishing, www.greenleaf-publishing.com/pdfs/ustanwad.pdf): 19-42.

Barrientos, S., C. Dolan and A. Tallontire (2001) *Gender and Ethical Trade: A Mapping of the Issues in African Horticulture* (Working Paper No. 26; Chatham, UK: NRI).

——, —— and —— (2003) 'A Gendered Value Chain Approach to Codes of Conduct in African Horticulture', *World Development* 31.9: 1,511-26.

Bendell, J., and D. Murphy (1999) *Partners in Time? Business, NGOs and Sustainable Development* (Discussion Paper 109; Geneva: UNRISD).

Blowfield, M. (2003a) 'CSR and Development: Is Business Appropriating Global Justice?', *Development* 47.3: 61-68.

—— (2003b) *Ethical Trade: The Negotiation of a Global Ethic* (DPhil thesis; Falmer, UK: University of Sussex).

Courville, S. (2003) 'Social Accountability Audits: Challenging of Defending Democratic Governance?', *Law and Policy* 25.3: 269-97.

Dolan, C., M. Opondo and S. Smith (2003) *Gender, Rights and Participation in the Kenya Cut Flower Industry* (NRI Report No. 2768; Chatham, UK: NRI).

East African Standard (2003) 'Stop Labour Turf Wars', *East African Standard*, 3 March 2003; gate.cosatu.org.za/pipermail/news/2003-March/000161.html.

FIAN (2004) 'Kenya: Weak Laws for a Strong Industry', www.fian.de/fian/index.php?option=content&task=view&id=178&Itemid=50, accessed 26 May 2005.

Freeman, R.E. (1984) *Strategic Management: A Stakeholder Approach* (Boston, MA: Pitman).

Green, M. (2002) 'Valentines a Thorny Issue for Kenya Flower Workers', Reuters, 14 February 2002; www.planetark.com/avantgo/dailynewsstory.cfm?newsid=14515.

---

7 The costs of auditing are borne by cut flower producers. The lower cost of the HEBI PSA pre-audit and audit (US$1,200.00) could therefore increase code adoption if HEBI achieves market recognition.

Heins, B. (2004) 'The Role of Labour Unions in the Process Towards Sustainable Consumption and Production, Final Report to the UNEP', www.uneptie.org/outreach/business/labour.htm, accessed 26 May 2005.

Hennock, M. (2002) 'Kenya's Flower Farms Flourish', *BBC News*, 14 February, news.bbc.co.uk/1/hi/business/1820515.stm, accessed 26 May 2005.

Hill, C.W.L., and T.M. Jones (1992) 'Stakeholder-Agency Theory', *Journal of Management Studies* 29: 131-54.

Lloyd, N. (2002) 'Women Tell of Rape in Farms', *The East African Standard*, 9 March 2002 (allafrica.com/stories/200203090138.html).

Mwai, R. (2004) Report on the *National Stakeholders Workshop: Horticulture in Kenya*, Safari Park Hotel, 12 February 2004.

Mwarania, B. (2004) 'Census of Flower Farms in Kenya', unpublished data.

Tallontire, A., C. Dolan, S. Barrientos and S. Smith (forthcoming) 'Gender Value Chains in African Horticulture', *Development in Practice*.

Utting, P. (2002) 'Regulating Business via Multistakeholder Initiatives: A Preliminary Assessment', in *UNRISD Voluntary Approaches to Corporate Responsibility: Readings and a Resource Guide* (Geneva: UNRISD): 61-130.

The Cocoa Industry
and Child Labour*

Elliot J. Schrage
Council on Foreign Relations, USA

Anthony P. Ewing
Columbia University, USA

Reports of forced child labour on the cocoa farms of Côte d'Ivoire surfaced in 2000 and quickly became an important business issue for a number of prominent companies. Media coverage and the threat of regulatory action mobilised the international cocoa industry to collaborate with other stakeholders to eliminate the worst forms of child labour from cocoa production. The international cocoa industry moved from a refusal to acknowledge serious labour problems in the global cocoa supply chain, to acknowledgement, and a public commitment to act to address the problems. The experience of the cocoa industry provides a number of lessons for executives, advocates and policy-makers seeking to promote labour standards. Industry participants sought the participation of multiple stakeholders, defined standards by referencing international law, and sought reliable information from the field. This case also demonstrates that pressure on consumer brands, strategic government intervention and geographic concentration facilitates collaborative action.

● Cocoa
● Child labour
● Forced labour
● Côte d'Ivoire
● Human rights
● Cocoa Industry Protocol
● International Cocoa Initiative

Elliot J. Schrage is a lawyer and business adviser. He is currently Adjunct Professor at Columbia's Business and Law Schools and Bernard L. Schwartz Senior Fellow in Business and Foreign Policy at the Council on Foreign Relations in New York. He previously served as Senior Vice President for Global Affairs at Gap, Inc.

✉ 2741 Divisadero Street, San Francisco, CA 94123, USA

🖥 schrage@post.harvard.edu

Anthony P. Ewing is a lawyer and management consultant based in New York. He is a lecturer in law at Columbia University, where he co-teaches the graduate seminar, 'Transnational Business and Human Rights'.

✉ 451 Walton Road, Maplewood, NJ 07040, USA

🖥 aewing@law.columbia.edu

* Original research for this paper was supported by a grant from the United States Department of State under the auspices of the University of Iowa Center for Human Rights. An earlier version of this paper was published as a case study in Schrage 2004: 131.

R EPORTS OF SLAVE LABOUR ON COCOA FARMS SURFACED AS EARLY AS 1998, WHEN an Ivorian newspaper reported the widespread practice of importing and indenturing Malian boys for fieldwork on Ivorian plantations (USDOS 1999). The United States Department of State reported an initial estimate of 15,000 Malian children working on Ivorian cocoa and coffee plantations (USDOS 2001). The child workers, many of whom were under 12 years of age, were sold into indentured servitude for US$140 and worked 12 hour days for US$135 to 189 per year.

Côte d'Ivoire is the world's leading cocoa producer, typically supplying more than 40% of the cocoa consumed worldwide. In 2001, Côte d'Ivoire exported 1.4 million tons of cocoa beans.[1] Cocoa production employed more than 7 million people on 450,000 Ivorian cocoa farms, and cocoa exports accounted for a third of the country's export earnings. Unlike the European and North American markets that consume most of the cocoa, Côte d'Ivoire and its neighbours rank among the world's least developed countries.[2] Average per capita GDP (gross domestic product) for Côte d'Ivoire's 16 million people is US$1,490.

In September 2000, a British television documentary reported that hundreds of thousands of children in Burkina Faso, Mali and Togo were being purchased from their parents and sold as slaves to cocoa farmers in neighbouring Côte d'Ivoire. The documentary included claims that slavery existed on as many as 90% of Ivorian cocoa farms. According to subsequent media accounts, children as young as six years old were forced to work 80–100 hour weeks without pay, suffered from malnutrition, and were subject to beatings and other abuse.

The media spotlight prompted Ivorian government officials to blame the international cocoa industry for keeping prices too low to ensure an adequate standard of living for Ivorian cocoa farmers. In its 2000 report on human rights practices in Côte d'Ivoire, the US Department of State observed, 'Children regularly are trafficked into the country from neighbouring countries and sold into forced labour' (USDOS 2001). The UK called for West African states to sign a treaty establishing a legal framework for combating slavery and forced labour, and the British Foreign Office created a task force of governments, industry and NGOs to address forced labour in the cocoa industry. The following month, in June 2001, Knight Ridder Newspapers in the United States profiled cocoa farm slaves between the ages of 12 and 16, and reported on one Côte d'Ivoire farmer who had been prosecuted in Côte d'Ivoire for mistreating 19 boys from Mali and holding them in abysmal conditions (*Knight Ridder/Tribune Business News* 2001).

The public allegations of child slavery would reverberate throughout the global cocoa industry, prompting major cocoa brands to reassess their sphere of influence over and responsibility for human rights conditions in the cocoa supply chain.

---

1 A coup attempt in September 2002 triggered a civil war between the Ivorian government in the south of Côte d'Ivoire and rebel forces in the north. The conflict disrupted cocoa production for the 2002–03 harvest season. The violent conflict displaced more than 1 million people within Côte d'Ivoire and caused more than 150,000 immigrants to flee to neighbouring countries. A peace agreement between the government and rebels was reached in January 2003, but fell apart in October 2004 with renewed violence by government and rebel forces, and involving French peacekeepers, which triggered a new wave of refugees. Overall cocoa exports have remained steady, but ongoing instability, disruptions in the cocoa harvest and cocoa bean transportation, and ethnic violence targeting immigrant populations involved in the cocoa industry threaten Côte d'Ivoire's position as the leading cocoa producer (Kahn 2004).

2 Côte d'Ivoire ranks 161st out of 175 countries on the United Nations Development Programme (UNDP) Human Development Index (UNDP 2003).

The global cocoa supply chain

Most cocoa is grown on small farms of less than 6 hectares. Cocoa bean production is labour-intensive and overwhelmingly a family enterprise.[3] In Côte d'Ivoire, for example, the average farm has five workers, and four or five are the former's family members (IITA 2002: 20).

The cocoa supply chain includes many intermediaries between the farmer and consumer. Small farmers typically sell their cocoa harvest to local middlemen for cash. The middlemen work under contract for local exporters, who, in turn, sell cocoa to international traders and the major international cocoa brands. The US-based agricultural trading companies Archer Daniels Midland (ADM) and Cargill, private companies Guittard Chocolate Company and Blommer Chocolate Co., and the Swiss multinationals Nestlé, and Barry and Callebaut AG, are the largest chocolate processing companies.[4] ADM and Cargill own processing plants in Côte d'Ivoire.

The global market price for cocoa beans, averaging 78 cents per pound in August 2004, is determined on the future markets of the London Cocoa Terminal Market and the New York Cocoa Exchange. Of course, after every level in the supply chain earns a profit, farmers receive substantially lower prices per pound than the price on global markets.

North America and Western Europe consume two-thirds of global cocoa production. Nestlé, the US companies Mars, Inc. and Hershey Foods, and Britain's Cadbury Schweppes are the leading chocolate producers.[5]

The human rights at issue

Allegations of abusive conditions on cocoa farms raised human rights issues for governments and cocoa industry participants. The human rights at issue are widely accepted international standards prohibiting child labour, forced labour and trafficking in persons.

Prohibited child labour

Child labour is common in the agricultural sector and widespread in countries where cocoa is grown.[6] The International Labour Organisation (ILO) estimates that there are 378,000 working children in Côte d'Ivoire alone (ILO 2001a). When allegations of child labour on cocoa farms were first made, Côte d'Ivoire was not a party to the ILO Minimum Age Convention[7] and Ivorian minimum age laws did not conform to international legal standards.

---

3 Year-round work on a cacao farm includes clearing underbrush and applying pesticides and fungicides. Cocoa bean harvesting entails cutting the pods from the trees, slicing them open, scooping out the beans, covering them in baskets or on mats to ferment, and then drying the beans in the sun. There are around 40 cocoa beans in one cacao pod, and about 400 cocoa beans are used to make a pound of chocolate.

4 The gross sales figures for these companies are: Nestlé (US$71 billion, 2003), Cargill (US$63 billion, 2004), ADM (US$36 billion, 2004), Barry Callebaut AG (US$3 billion, 2004). The financial statements for Blommer Chocolate Co. and Guittard Chocolate are not publicly available. The diversified companies do not report publicly on revenues attributable to cocoa sales alone.

5 Recent gross sales figures are: Nestlé (US$71 billion, 2003), Mars, Inc. (US$17 billion, est., 2003), Cadbury Schweppes (US$11.5 billion, 2003) and Hershey Foods (US$4 billion, 2003). Mars, Inc. and Hershey Foods control two-thirds of the US$13 billion US chocolate market. In 2000, the United States consumed 3.3 billion pounds of chocolate.

6 The ILO estimates that 70% of child labour occurs in the agricultural sector (ILO 2002: xi).

7 ILO Convention (No. 138) Concerning Minimum Age for Admission to Employment (1973) [hereinafter 'ILO C138'].

Under Ivorian law, children over the age of 14 are allowed to work as long as the work is not dangerous and the children have parental consent. The legal minimum age for agricultural work is 12. Local labour law limits the hours of workers under 18. In practice, children often work on family farms and in the informal economy.

Widely accepted international labour standards, such as those contained in ILO and United Nations conventions, prohibit any form of work by children younger than 12.[8] Under international conventions, developing countries may permit the employment of children in 'family and small-scale holdings producing for local consumption and not regularly employing hired workers.'[9]

Permanent workers younger than 12 on cocoa farms would fall short of international standards. Family children who perform more than 'light work' or whose work interferes with compulsory education also classify as prohibited child labourers under ILO standards. Primary education in Côte d'Ivoire is compulsory but unenforced, particularly in rural areas. Primary education usually ends at age 13 (USDOS 2001). Since cocoa is produced predominantly for export, international standards make no exception to minimum age standards due to the family or small-scale nature of cocoa farms.

Forced child labour

Employing cocoa workers without their consent or not allowing workers to leave farms voluntarily constitutes forced labour, a form of slavery.[10] Côte d'Ivoire has ratified the ILO Forced Labour Convention[11] and forced labour is prohibited under Ivorian law.

Côte d'Ivoire and most other states have made international commitments to eliminate the worst forms of child labour, including forced labour. In 1999, 132 countries adopted the ILO Convention on the Worst Forms of Child Labour[12] which calls on states to 'take immediate and effective measures to prohibit and eliminate all forms of slavery . . . and forced or compulsory labour', as well as 'work which is likely to harm the health, safety or morals of children, determined by national laws or regulations'.[13] The nature of the work performed on cocoa farms by anyone under the age of 18, even if voluntary, may qualify as prohibited child labour under this Convention.[14] Growing cocoa involves

---

8 Article 2 of ILO C138 sets the minimum age for employment or work as the age of completion of compulsory schooling or 15 years, whichever is lower, though there are a number of exceptions available to state signatories. For countries with developing economies and educational systems, the minimum employment age can be set at 14 years; ILO C138, art. 5, para. 3. The United Nations Convention on the Rights of the Child (1989) defines 'child' as anyone under 18 and affirms the right of the child to be protected from economic exploitation and any work 'likely to be hazardous or to interfere with the child's education, or to be harmful to the child's health or physical, mental, spiritual, moral or social development'; Art. 32.

9 ILO C138, art. 5, para. 3. States are permitted to eliminate entire categories of employment from the scope of the Convention, including 'family and small-scale holdings producing for local consumption and not regularly employing hired workers'. Also, 'light work' is permitted for children as young as 12 who have not completed compulsory schooling; *Ibid*. art. 7.

10 The prohibition of slavery, of course, is a fundamental and universal human rights standard contained in the Universal Declaration of Human Rights (1948), art. 4, the International Covenant on Civil and Political Rights (1966), art. 8, and the African Charter on Human and People's Rights (1986), art. 5, among others.

11 ILO Convention (No. 29) Concerning Forced or Compulsory Labour (1930) [hereinafter 'ILO C29']. Forced labour is 'all work or service which is exacted from any person under the menace of any penalty and for which the said person has not offered himself voluntarily'.

12 ILO Convention (No. 182) Concerning the Prohibition and Immediate Action for the Elimination of the Worst Forms of Child Labor (1999) [hereinafter 'ILO C182']. Cote d'Ivoire ratified ILO C182 in February 2003.

13 ILO C182, art. 3.

14 Article 2 of ILO C182 provides that 'the term "child" shall apply to all persons under the age of 18'. For any type of employment or work that is 'likely to jeopardize the health, safety or morals of young

long hours in the sun performing physically demanding work. Workers often use primitive tools, travel great distances, and are exposed to pesticides and chemical fertilisers, poisonous and disease-carrying insects and reptiles (Save the Children Canada 2003). The US Department of State estimates that there are 109,000 child labourers working in hazardous conditions on cocoa farms, some of whom are forced or indentured workers, but most work on family farms or with their parents (USDOS 2003).

Trafficking in persons

A key allegation in the accounts from West Africa was that children were not only forced to work and were mistreated on cocoa farms, but that they were also trafficked by cocoa farmers and their agents.

UNICEF estimates that hundreds of thousands of children are sold as slaves each year (UNICEF 2002: vii) and that 200,000 children are trafficked through West and Central Africa annually (HRW 2003: 8).[15] The most common forms of trafficking in the region are the voluntary placement of children by parents with a third party for a set price or for a set period of time during which the intermediary collects the wages paid by the employer (ILO 2001a: 2-3). Bonded labour, or the exchange of child labour as repayment of a debt, while a problem in some countries, is not as prevalent in West Africa. Child trafficking is driven by poverty, poor education and weak or non-existent punishment for traffickers, and facilitated by African traditions of migration and the placement of children with family members. Migrant labour in Côte d'Ivoire historically comes from Burkina Faso and Mali, two of the poorest countries in the world.

West African governments have begun to address child trafficking through regional and bilateral initiatives.[16] In September 2000, Côte d'Ivoire and Mali signed the first bilateral agreement in the region to establish formal procedures for co-operation against child trafficking.[17] Between 1998 and 2002, more than 800 Malian children working on Ivorian plantations were repatriated by Côte d'Ivoire. Many of these children had been working on small farms.

Ivorian law does not prohibit trafficking in persons, but the government prosecutes trafficking under existing laws against forced labour and the kidnapping of children.[18]

---

persons' the minimum age is 18 years also; ILO C138, art. 2. National legislation defines the types of work subject to this standard, and the minimum age can be 16 under certain conditions.

15 Trafficking is not solely a child labour issue: 'trafficking violates the rights of children long before their actual labour begins' (UNICEF 2002: 7). As defined in international instruments, trafficking in persons is: 'the recruitment, transportation, transfer, harbouring or receipt of persons, by means of the threat or use of force or other forms of coercion, of abduction, of fraud, of deception, of the abuse of power or of a position of vulnerability or of the giving or receiving of payments or benefits to achieve the consent of a person having control over another person for the purpose of exploitation'. Protocol to Prevent, Suppress and Punish Trafficking in Persons, Especially Women and Children, supplementing the United Nations Convention against Transnational Organized Crime (2000); Optional Protocol to the Convention on the Rights of the Child on the Sale of Children, Child Prostitution and Child Pornography (2000). Côte d'Ivoire is not a party to either of these protocols.

16 Formal governmental efforts to address child trafficking in the region began in 2000 with the Libreville Common Platform for Action. *Common Platform for Action of the Sub-Regional Consultation on the Development of Strategies to fight Child Trafficking for Exploitation Labour Purposes in West and Central Africa*, 22–24 February 2000 (signed in Libreville, Gabon).

17 Co-operation Agreement between the Republic of Côte d'Ivoire and the Republic of Mali on Combating Trans-border Trafficking of Children, 1 September 2000.

18 In September 2001, for example, a local Ivorian court in the southern cocoa region convicted a Togo citizen of trafficking three ten-year-old children to work on Ivorian farms, sentenced him to three years' imprisonment, and ordered him to leave the country for five years after his release. At least nine traffickers were arrested and 100 children rescued in 2002; however, all anti-trafficking law

Response of the global cocoa industry

Even though child trafficking and forced labour in the agricultural sector of West Africa had been a subject of concern among international development organisations and within the region since at least 1995, no cocoa industry brand or processor had publicly identified or taken measures to address the labour issues in cocoa production before abusive labour conditions generated media attention. Over a relatively short period, the international cocoa industry moved from refusing to acknowledge serious labour issues in its supply chain to acknowledging them and making a public commitment to act to address the problems.

Initially, the major European and American cocoa brands denied responsibility for conditions in the cocoa fields, arguing that they had been unaware of the problems or that the cocoa supply chain was too complex to guarantee working practices on every farm.

> [W]e have been visiting the Ivory Coast for decades and working closely with many cocoa farmers. In all that time, we have simply not come across such practices. We are confident that, while illegal practices may exist, this is on a very limited scale indeed and confined to certain areas (John Newman, Director of the British Biscuit, Cake, Confectionery, and Chocolate Alliance [BCCCA], June 2001).

> [N]o one, repeat no one, had ever heard of this. Your instinct is that Hershey should have known. But the fact is we didn't know (Robert M. Reese, Senior Vice President of Hershey Foods, June 2001).

When confronted with the allegations, no company was able to guarantee that its cocoa supply chain was child labour-free, since most companies sourced at least some cocoa from Côte d'Ivoire.

Pressure for responsibility

Media reports connecting their valuable consumer brands with the mistreatment of children posed a clear threat to corporate reputation and sales. Another reason for the industry's quick turnaround was the credible threat of regulatory action. United States trade law forbids the import of products made with slave labour and an Executive Order prohibits federal agencies from purchasing goods made with forced child labour.[19] Following the slavery allegations, the US government formally considered adding cocoa from Côte d'Ivoire to the prohibited list of goods. This move would have been a significant blow to the cocoa industry. In June 2001, legislation was proposed in the United States Congress to create a 'no child slave labour' labelling requirement for all cocoa products.

The global chocolate and cocoa industry, caught off-guard by the slavery allegations and the threat of regulation, sought to protect its business and define its sphere of responsibility for labour conditions in the cocoa fields. The United States' Chocolate Manufacturers Association (CMA) opposed the proposed labelling schemes,[20] and before Congress voted on labelling legislation, the cocoa industry announced an initiative 'to

---

enforcement efforts in Côte d'Ivoire have ceased since the civil unrest that began in September 2002 (USDOS 2003).

19 Trade Act of 1930, § 307, 19 USC § 1307 (1997) (prohibiting United States' imports of products created with 'forced or indentured child labor'); Exec. Order No. 13126, 64 Fed. Reg. 32,383 (12 June 1999). Chocolate and cocoa products are not on the list of applicable goods.

20 According to the CMA, '[a] "slave free" label would hurt the people it is intended to help because it could lead to a boycott of Ivorian cocoa'. *CMA Lobbies Against 'Slave Free' Label Proposal*, Candy Industry, 1 August 2001, at 13.

address the workers' rights issues recently identified by the government of the Ivory Coast':

> As an industry, we strongly condemn abusive labour practices, and our goal is to be part of the worldwide effort to solve this problem . . . Given the importance of cocoa farming to the well-being of the people of the Ivory Coast and throughout the region, we believe it is critical to continue to support the vast majority of family farms there by doing everything possible to improve labour conditions (Chocolate Manufacturers Association, press release, 22 June 2001).

As a first step, the major cocoa brands committed to funding a survey on the ground in West Africa to determine the full extent of forced child labour and trafficking in cocoa production. At the same time, the industry reinforced the principle that states have primary responsibility for enforcing human rights by calling on governments to 'investigate and eradicate any criminal child labour activity'.[21]

The Cocoa Industry Protocol

The cocoa industry made concrete its public commitment to respond to labour abuses by launching a multi-stakeholder initiative. On 19 September 2001, the CMA and the World Cocoa Foundation signed a Protocol committing themselves and their members to a series of steps to eliminate the worst forms of child labour in cocoa production. The Cocoa Industry Protocol (CIP) provides for 'the development of a credible, mutually acceptable system of industry-wide global standards, along with independent monitoring and reporting, to identify and eliminate any use of the worst forms of child labour in the growing and processing of cocoa beans' (ILO 2001b). Eight chief executives of major chocolate brands and cocoa processors expressed their 'personal support' for the CIP,[22] and the CIP was endorsed by the intergovernmental International Cocoa Organisation (ICO) and two European trade associations.[23]

The CIP was notable for referencing specific international labour standards, calling for independent monitoring and setting an aggressive timetable for implementation.[24] The CIP calls for compliance with ILO Convention (No. 182) Concerning the Prohibition and Immediate Action for the Elimination of the Worst Forms of Child Labour.[25] Industry, government and non-governmental participants subsequently created a Broad Consultative Group (BCG) to work collaboratively with the ILO to implement the CIP. The CIP participants emphasised the importance of eliminating all forced labour, in addition

---

21 International Cocoa Council Resolution on Agricultural Working Practices, 10 July 2001, www.icco. org/press/010620resolution.htm.

22 The chief executives of Guittard Chocolate Company, M&M/Mars, Inc., World's Finest Chocolate, Inc., Archer Daniels Midland Company, Nestlé Chocolate and Confections USA, Blommer Chocolate Company, Hershey Food Corporation and Barry Callebaut AG signed an expression of support for the Protocol.

23 Association of the Chocolate, Biscuits and Confectionery Industries of the European Union (COABISCO) and the European Cocoa Association (ECA).

24 The CIP called for: (a) a survey of the affected areas; (b) an advisory council to oversee the survey; (c) a consultative group comprising industry, non-governmental organisations, government agencies, and labour groups; (d) a pilot programme; (e) a monitoring group; (f) an international foundation; and (g) public certification that cocoa used in chocolate or related products has been grown and processed without forced child labour. Under the timetable established in the CIP, a joint action programme to establish independent monitoring and public reporting would be agreed to by May 2002, followed by industry-wide voluntary standards of public certification by 1 July 2005.

25 The Protocol incorporated by reference ILO C182 in its entirety. 'Protocol for the Growing and Processing of Cocoa Beans and their Derivative Products in a Manner that Complies with ILO Convention 182 Concerning the Prohibition and Immediate Action for the Elimination of the Worst Forms of Child Labor' (19 September 2001).

to the worst forms of child labour, and referenced ILO Convention (No. 29) Concerning Forced or Compulsory Labour.

The adoption of the CIP meant that global cocoa companies acknowledged their ability, collectively, to influence actors beyond their own operations and accepted a degree of responsibility for labour conditions in the cocoa supply chain.

> [W]e need to be permanently concerned with where cocoa comes from, the impact of cocoa on the environment and how the workers are treated. That's where the industry has changed, permanently and forever (Larry Graham, President of the CMA, October 2001).

Information gathering

Efforts in other industries to address supply chain labour standards have demonstrated that a critical first step for any collaborative initiative is obtaining reliable and credible information on local conditions (Schrage 2004). Under the CIP, the cocoa industry and its partners devoted resources first to gathering information from the field on the nature and dimension of the violations. The International Institute for Tropical Agriculture (IITA) surveyed labour conditions on cocoa farms in West Africa.[26]

The IITA survey helped to define the magnitude of the labour abuses and the categories of child workers at greatest risk. The IITA estimated that 625,000 children under 18 work on cocoa farms in Côte d'Ivoire (IITA 2002: 16). The vast majority of these children are the farmers' family members. The IITA found that: (a) tens of thousands of child workers in the Côte d'Ivoire cocoa sector are at high risk of trafficking and forced labour, not hundreds of thousands of child slaves as reported in initial media accounts; (b) many child workers perform the work voluntarily; (c) child trafficking is just as likely to occur within Côte d'Ivoire as from neighbouring countries; and (d) child labour is employed mostly by Ivorians as opposed to immigrant farmers. IITA's fieldwork revealed that salaried child workers and child workers with no family tie to the farmer are the most vulnerable to the worst forms of child labour.[27] According to IITA, the recruitment and employment of children from outside the family as permanent salaried workers is relatively uncommon.

None of the children surveyed reported that their parents had been paid or that they had been taken against their will; all reported being informed in advance of the work to be done on cocoa farms and having agreed to leave home for the promise of a better life. While more than 80% of the child workers reported being 'satisfied' or 'somewhat satisfied' with their current situation, one-third stated they were not free to leave their place of employment. Ivorian salaried child workers reported being paid less than adults while working the same number of hours: approximately six hours per day, six days a week. Farmers generally provided lodging and meals for salaried child workers.

The IITA surveys encountered a number of unsalaried children with no family tie to the household working in some capacity on cocoa farms.[28] IITA estimates that there are twice as many of these child workers on cocoa farms than salaried child workers.

The IITA survey also found family child workers on cocoa farms working in conditions detrimental to their health and welfare. The work children perform on cocoa farms includes pesticide application, clearing underbrush with a machete, carrying heavy

---

26 In February and March 2002, IITA surveyed cocoa farmers and workers from 1,500 farm households in 250 Côte d'Ivoire villages. In addition, IITA conducted community surveys in 15 Côte d'Ivoire villages to collect qualitative information on child labour (IITA 2002).

27 In Côte d'Ivoire, IITA estimated that there were 5,120 salaried child workers, or 8% of the estimated 66,720 salaried workers.

28 IITA estimates that there are 12,000 children under 18 assisting cocoa production on 9,000 Côte d'Ivoire farms.

loads, and using a machete to open the cocoa pods. According to IITA, almost 60,000 children under 15 are engaged in all cocoa-related tasks.

> The picture that emerges is of a sector with stagnant technology, low yields, and an increasing demand for unskilled workers trapped in a circle of poverty. Salaried child workers were most clearly trapped in a vicious circle. The majority of these children had never been to school and were earning subsistence wages, forced into this labour by economic circumstances. Most of these children are from the drier savannah areas of West Africa, where family livelihoods are inherently uncertain and households are forced into risk-reducing livelihood strategies, including sending adolescents to cocoa plantations to work (IITA 2002: 22).

The CMA viewed the IITA study findings as confirmation of 'the need to address the safety of children on cocoa farms and the economic well-being of cocoa farming families'.[29]

The field survey confirmed the practice of forced child labour and child trafficking in the cocoa supply chain, identified salaried child workers and child workers with no family tie to the farmer as the most vulnerable to abuse, and highlighted the potentially hazardous working conditions, independent of child trafficking and forced labour, of the 60,000 children under 14 performing all the tasks of cocoa production.

The International Cocoa Initiative

In July 2002, the global cocoa industry, in partnership with labour unions and non-governmental organisations, established the International Cocoa Initiative (ICI) to: (a) support field projects; (b) act as a clearinghouse for best practices; (c) conduct a joint research programme; and (d) develop a means of monitoring and public reporting under the CIP.[30]

Evaluating the Cocoa Industry Protocol and the International Cocoa Initiative

Under the terms of the Protocol, industry participants have committed by July 2005 to establish credible standards of public certification that cocoa production is free of the worst forms of child labour. CIP participants are working with the ILO and the governments of Ghana and Côte d'Ivoire to design and implement a certification system comprising child labour monitoring, a government-issued certificate and independent verification by third parties. Pilots of the monitoring system were scheduled to begin in Ghana and Côte d'Ivoire in late 2004.

In 2004, the ICI planned to launch pilot programmes in a limited number of communities in Ghana and Côte d'Ivoire to address child labour using local NGOs as intermediaries. According to the ICI, by 2005, the pilot communities will be implementing concrete activities.

Increased international awareness of child trafficking, forced labour and prohibited child labour in cocoa production has accelerated local government initiatives to combat these abuses in West Africa. On December 2001, the Economic Community of West African States (ECOWAS) adopted a Declaration and Plan of Action against Trafficking

---

29 CMA, 'Global Chocolate, Cocoa Industry Responding to Challenges Outlined in Labour Practices Survey', press release, 26 July 2002.
30 World Cocoa Foundation, 'Global Chocolate, Cocoa Industry and Stakeholders Establish Foundation, International Cocoa Initiative—Working Towards Responsible Labor Standards for Cocoa Growing', Press Release, 1 July 2002.

in Persons calling on member states to criminalise trafficking, protect and support victims, increase co-operation among border control agencies, establish national task forces, and ratify the principal international instruments on trafficking.[31] Côte d'Ivoire has ratified both the ILO Minimum Age Convention and the ILO Convention on the Worst Forms of Child Labour. Côte d'Ivoire and its neighbours have taken some bilateral steps to address child trafficking, but these efforts have not advanced since the Ivorian civil war began in 2002.

In 2003, the government of Côte d'Ivoire and the ILO announced the West African Project Against Abusive Child Labour in Commercial Agriculture (WACAP). Funded by the US Department of Labour and the cocoa industry, WACAP pilot programmes designed and managed by the ILO will address abusive child labour and forced labour by increasing farmer awareness, improving schools and providing better social services to families.

Within a year of the signing of the Protocol, the political situation in Côte d'Ivoire deteriorated, leading to the outbreak of civil war in September 2002. The war killed more than 3,000 people, displaced a million, and disrupted both the cocoa industry and the world cocoa market. Political violence in Côte d'Ivoire has weakened government law enforcement capacity in government-held areas, prevented northern workers from reaching the cocoa fields in the south, and halted government anti-trafficking efforts. A January 2003 ceasefire fell apart in October 2004 with a new wave of fighting. Not surprisingly, these developments have presented major obstacles to progress on the initiative, although the cocoa industry reports some progress on programmes to address labour issues in areas of relative stability.

Child trafficking and forced labour continue in the cocoa producing regions of West Africa. The US Department of State reports the ongoing trafficking of children into Côte d'Ivoire and estimates that 109,000 child labourers work in hazardous conditions on cocoa farms. Some of these children are forced or indentured workers, but 70% work on family farms or with their parents (USDOS 2004).

The principal critique of the CIP when it was announced was its narrow scope. Industry critics, while supporting the CIP as an important first step, argue that the initiative fails to address the underlying causes of child labour and exploitative working conditions. The International Labour Rights Fund (ILRF), a US-based advocacy group, faulted the CIP for failing to specify international minimum age or other core labour standards and for failing to ensure a fair price for farmers. ILRF also criticised the voluntary nature of the CIP, calling for a 'system of mandatory reporting, monitoring, and certification through national and international law'.[32] The ILRF's own investigation found the continuing practice of trafficked child labour supplied by labour brokers to cocoa farmers during the cocoa harvest season.[33] ILRF and other advocates question the progress made implementing the CIP and have called for individual cocoa industry participants to make changes and conduct training and monitoring in their own supply chains (ILRF 2004).

For the time being, the CIP and related industry initiatives have reduced public pressure for legislative or regulatory intervention by cocoa importing countries.

---

31 ECOWAS, Declaration on the Fight Against Trafficking in Persons (12 December 2001).

32 ILRF, 'Statement on Industry Protocol Regarding Use of Child Labor in West African Cocoa Farms', 1 May 2002.

33 According to the ILRF, 'Child slaves are used on cocoa plantations all over [Côte d'Ivoire] without any observable programs to stop the practice . . . Whatever the chocolate manufacturers claim to be doing about this, we cannot leave a problem as serious as child slavery to voluntary private efforts' (Price 2002).

Lessons from the cocoa industry's experience

The CIP and the ICI reinforce lessons learned from earlier voluntary initiatives to address labour standards in other industries, such as sporting goods, apparel, coffee and toys (Schrage 2004). For example, industry participants sought the participation of multiple stakeholders from both inside and outside the industry in order to distribute responsibilities, costs and risks and to gain access to a wide range of expertise. The labour standards at issue were defined in the CIP by referencing widely accepted international legal standards and the partners devoted resources first to gathering information from the field on the true nature and dimension of the violations.

The experience of the cocoa industry in West Africa provides a number of lessons for executives, advocates and policy-makers seeking to promote labour standards through voluntary initiatives in Africa and elsewhere.

Effective risk management means understanding your supply chain

The major cocoa traders and brands easily could have anticipated the labour issues in the global cocoa supply chain. Child labour is common in the agricultural sector, widespread in the countries where cocoa is grown, and reports of child trafficking and forced labour in Côte d'Ivoire had been a subject of concern among development organisations for at least three years before the first media reports of child slavery on cocoa farms. The failure to exercise appropriate 'due diligence' left companies open to accusations with the potential to hurt their business and reputation, and unprepared to respond quickly. Corporate assertions of ignorance and the complexity of the supply chain proved to be inadequate responses.

The geographic concentration of a supply chain facilitates industry-wide initiatives

The geographic concentration of the global cocoa supply chain made launching the cocoa initiatives feasible. Côte d'Ivoire produces approximately 40% of the world's trade in cocoa, and was quickly identified as the primary sourcing market at risk for forced child labour. The global cocoa industry made the logical strategic decision to launch its programme in that country. Even if the programme never reaches other sourcing markets, implementing it effectively in Côte d'Ivoire and its neighbours could achieve significant improvements in labour standards in cocoa production.

The obstacles facing the industry in Côte d'Ivoire are substantial. But the benefits of launching a programme in one sourcing market, focusing on one specific issue and dealing with one set of local government institutions and national labour standards, are tremendous. Geographic concentration also makes it easier to identify qualified monitors, train them on local conditions and local standards, and build bridges to qualified partners.

Partnerships with expert organisations are essential for private regulatory initiatives to succeed

The CIP and the ICI demonstrate the need for effective partnerships between the private sector, government, international and civil society organisations to achieve sustainable change in business practices. The CIP and the ICI have relied on the government of Côte d'Ivoire, the ILO, USAID, the IITA, Free the Slaves, and other organisations as partners, collaborators and resources.

These partnerships serve several purposes. First, they reinforce the credibility of the initiative. The involvement not only of governmental and inter-governmental organisations, but also of independent NGOs in the design and oversight of the Protocol, has helped the cocoa industry overcome scepticism about the seriousness of its efforts. Second, they have brought financial support to the initiative from governments. Third, the network of NGO partners has helped the CIP signatories and the ICI to identify resources to perform field research and training.

Consumer demand for higher standards is limited

Consumer pressure was insufficient to spark industry collaboration to address child labour in the cocoa supply chain. Though public scrutiny was the spark for industry action, the experience of the cocoa industry suggests that industry responded much more to the threat of government intervention than it did to market pressure. Demand for 'fair trade' chocolate, for example, has remained relatively small.[34]

Consumer brands are the most effective leverage point to push for collaborative standard-setting initiatives

If market forces play only a limited role in raising labour standards in the cocoa supply chain, why should the role of major chocolate brands be so valuable in realising improvements? The answer reveals the important role the brands play in the cocoa supply chain. Even if the direct impact of consumer pressure on sales and profits is limited, global cocoa brands value their public reputations, and the premium such positive reputations often bring in the capital markets. Moreover, even if the threat from consumer action may be limited, the challenge presented by government intervention was, in this case, perceived as serious. Consequently, the brands had an incentive to address the issue even if its direct impact on their sales appeared small.

Chocolate brands capture most of the value created in the cocoa supply chain. Any action that threatens that supply chain imposes the greatest burden on the brands, not the relatively anonymous suppliers. Influencing the assessment of those risks may be the most effective mechanism to alter supply chain practices.

Industry initiatives have the potential to define and enforce international legal standards

The incorporation in the CIP of specific international instruments overcomes the obstacle presented by local standards that fail to meet international standards, either on paper or in practice. Defining labour standards according to international law also avoids the criticism of encouraging a 'race to the bottom', often levelled at corporate human rights initiatives that make local law the default minimum standard (Ewing 2004). The

---

34 'Fair trade' chocolate has been sold in Europe for many years, but the market for such products proved insufficient to motivate the industry to examine its global sourcing practices in order to attract greater consumer interest. While demand for 'fair trade' production of cocoa is growing, it is unlikely any time soon to reach the point where it will account for a substantial percentage of worldwide cocoa production. To supply Fair Trade Certified™ cocoa, a cocoa grower must be a small farmer not dependent on hired labour and a member of a democratically organised farmer co-operative in which small farmers constitute a majority of the co-op's members. Fairtrade Labelling Organisation (FLO)'s international standards require cocoa producer organisations to adhere to national law, prohibit discrimination within co-operatives, and prohibit any forced or child labour in accordance with ILO legal standards (FLO, Fairtrade Standards for Cocoa, January 2003). There is no registered fair trade cocoa co-operative in Côte d'Ivoire.

CIP participants represent substantial leverage within the global cocoa industry, leverage that could be used to promote government policies that adopt and enforce international labour standards. In this case, industry efforts in conjunction with foreign governments and international organisations prompted the Ivorian government to adopt international labour standards.

Strategic government intervention can enhance the effectiveness of industry initiatives to address labour standards

Unquestionably, the critical development that transformed industry concern into collaborative action was the introduction of legislation in the US Congress to require chocolate to bear labels based on the existence of child labour in cocoa sourcing markets. The industry was galvanised into reaching agreement with its critics and to identifying other partners only when faced with the prospect of government intervention in the United States and the United Kingdom. Continued government interest and support has been essential for the progress of the CIP and the ICI. Greater involvement by governments in cocoa-producing countries would strengthen the initiatives even further.

Voluntary initiatives to set labour standards are a second-best solution

The CIP emphasises the role of the local government to enforce its own labour laws to address violations and improve working conditions. National regulation and enforcement of local laws consistent with international labour standards are the most effective tools to stop child trafficking, eliminate forced and child labour, ensure freedom of association and enforce acceptable working conditions. Efforts by individual companies to date have had little measurable impact on labour standards on the ground. Efforts to build local enforcement capacity in cocoa-producing countries may be the most efficient way to improve labour standards for cocoa workers. Indeed, securing the partnership of the governments of Ghana and Côte d'Ivoire has been essential in designing the child labour certification scheme envisioned by the CIP.

Labour standard-setting initiatives fail in zones of conflict

It is an obvious final point: industry programmes to promote labour standards cannot succeed in situations of violent conflict. A government devoting its limited resources to fighting a civil war is unlikely to fulfil its obligations to enforce local labour standards. While Côte d'Ivoire and neighbouring countries have taken small steps to address child labour in the cocoa sector, civil unrest, lack of resources and the absence of political will on the part of local governments have outweighed any positive impact of the voluntary industry-led initiative to date. Ongoing civil unrest and ethnic tension in Côte d'Ivoire has the potential to permanently disrupt cocoa production there, prompt international cocoa processors to purchase cocoa beans elsewhere, reduce the country's export earnings, and lower even further the standard of living for most citizens. Any of these developments can deepen the extreme poverty that is a root cause of child labour in all its forms.

References

Ewing, A. (2004) 'Understanding the Global Compact Human Rights Principles', in United Nations Global Compact and the Office of the High Commissioner for Human Rights, *Embedding Human Rights into Business Practice* (New York: UN Global Compact Office): 28.

HRW (Human Rights Watch) (2003) *Borderline Slavery: Child Trafficking in Togo* (New York: HRW).

IITA (International Institute of Tropical Agriculture) (2002) *Child Labor in the Cocoa Sector of West Africa: A Synthesis of Findings in Cameroon, Côte d'Ivoire, Ghana, and Nigeria* (Croydon, UK: IITA).

ILO (International Labour Office) (2001a) *Combating Trafficking in Children for Labour Exploitation in West and Central Africa* (Geneva: ILO).

—— (2001b) 'Agreement to End Child Labour on Cocoa Farms', press release, 1 October 2001, www.ilo.org/public/english/bureau/inf/pr/2001/32.htm, 12 November 2003.

—— (2002) *A Future Without Child Labour* (Geneva: ILO).

ILRF (International Labor Rights Fund) (2004) *Chocolate and Child Slavery: Unfulfilled Promises of the Cocoa Industry* (Washington, DC: ILRF).

Kahn, J. (2004) 'The Chocolate War', *Fortune International*, 23 February 2004.

Knight Ridder/Tribune Business News (2001) 'Much of America's Sweets Made Possible through Slave Labor on Ivory Coast', *Knight Ridder/Tribune Business News*, 25 June 2001.

Price, E. (2002) 'Labor Group Demands US Ban on Imported Ivory Coast Cocoa', *Dow Jones*, 31 May 2002.

Save the Children Canada (2003) *Children Still in the Chocolate Trade: The Buying, Selling And Toiling of West African Child Workers in the Multibillion Dollar Industry* (Toronto: Save the Children Canada): 19-22.

Schrage, E. (2004) *Promoting International Worker Rights through Private Voluntary Initiatives: Public Relations or Public Policy?* (Iowa City, IA: University of Iowa Center for Human Rights).

UNDP (United Nations Development Fund) (2003) *Human Development Report, 2003* (New York: UNDP).

UNICEF (2002) *Child Trafficking in West Africa: Policy Responses* (Florence, Italy: UNICEF-Innocenti Insight).

USDOS (US Department of State) (1999) *Country Reports on Human Rights Practices for 1998: Côte d'Ivoire* (Washington, DC: USDOS).

—— (2001) *Country Reports on Human Rights Practices for 2000: Côte d'Ivoire* (Washington, DC: USDOS).

—— (2003) *Country Reports on Human Rights Practices for 2002: Côte d'Ivoire* (Washington, DC: USDOS).

—— (2004) *Country Reports on Human Rights Practices for 2003: Côte d'Ivoire* (Washington, DC: USDOS).

Why Teach Corporate Citizenship Differently?

Derick de Jongh

Centre for Corporate Citizenship, University of South Africa

Paul Prinsloo

Institute for Curriculum and Learning Development, University of South Africa

In this paper the impact of present business school curricula on corporate citizenship practices is questioned and the need for alternative corporate citizenship education is explored. We believe that education can redefine the role business plays in society. The paradoxes facing corporate citizenship in Africa challenges us to think (and teach) differently. For education to really make a difference in the way we perceive the responsibility of business, we propose a *critical* pedagogy for corporate citizenship. Critical corporate citizenship in Africa can contribute immensely towards effectively addressing the growing levels of unemployment, poverty, HIV/AIDS, corruption and crime. We conclude that, for education to really inform (and change) corporate citizenship practices in Africa, it should embrace a pedagogy of critique, possibility and engagement.

- Corporate social responsibility
- Consumerism
- Grand narratives
- Critical pedagogy
- Neocapitalism
- Africa

Dr **Derick de Jongh** is founding director of the Centre for Corporate Citizenship at the University of South Africa (Unisa). Derick completed his doctorate through the University of Pretoria in July 2003. The title of his dissertation was: 'Indicators of Corporate Social Performance in South Africa'.

AJH 1-74, PO Box 392, Unisa 0003, Republic of South Africa

djongd@unisa.ac.za

www.unisa.ac.za

Paul Prinsloo is a Learning Developer at the Institute for Curriculum and Learning Development at Unisa. He is enrolled for a DLitt et Phil at Unisa, exploring pedagogies of empowerment, possibility and hope.

TVW 4-69, PO Box 392, Unisa 0003, Republic of South Africa

prinsp@unisa.ac.za

www.unisa.ac.za

THE HEADLINE 'EQUATORIAL GUINEA'S OIL BOOM BENEFITS FEW' IN *THIS DAY* (Lister 2004: 4)[1] echoes the paradoxes facing corporate citizenship in Africa. While Africa needs investment and development, the investment comes at a cost and seems to benefit only a few. The challenges facing corporate citizenship in Africa involve messy, 'on the edge of chaos' (Calton and Payne 2003) scenarios where child labour, HIV/AIDS, 'Stark Poverty in a Sea of Oil and Diamonds' (Tleane 2003: 23), corruption and crime are rife. But what precisely do these societal ills have to do with business?

Zadek (2001: 2) says that, amid unfettered trade liberalisation, 'few have seriously faced up to the challenge of whether corporate citizenship can deliver sufficient social and environmental gains to reverse the underlying pattern of growing poverty, inequality, and environmental insecurity'. There is a great deal of cynicism in the corporate world and society in general about the social responsibility of corporations. On the one hand the corporate world demands proof that 'being good' adds monetary value to its portfolios, while, on the other hand, many stakeholders see corporate citizenship as mere window-dressing by companies to hide abusive practices. The business case tries to sell that 'it pays to be good', while society is demanding more and more that business 'be good—even if it doesn't pay'.

This paper proposes that traditional business curricula do *not* prepare business leaders sufficiently to critically reflect on present practices and come up with innovative and responsible decisions. There is a need to scout for alternative approaches that would better prepare them for the paradoxes and 'messiness' (Calton and Payne 2003) that await them. There is furthermore the notion that 'A Return to African Values' in business school curricula (Naidoo 2004: 2) will enhance corporate citizenship.

Education deals with 'images of that which is not yet' (Bloch 1970). While the present business school curricula emphasise acquiring competences in the canon of business management, it would seem as if the canon does not sufficiently and efficiently address the complex challenges facing business in Africa. Using the metaphor of 'that which is not yet', education should therefore enable learners 'to expand what it is to be human and contribute to the establishment of a just and compassionate community in which a project of possibility becomes the guiding principle of social order' (Simon 1987: 372).

In this paper we shall:

▶ Investigate concerns about the current business school curricula

▶ Explore some corporate citizenship paradoxes and 'grand narratives' (Lyotard 1984) facing business leaders

▶ Investigate the need for alternative approaches

Concerns about the current state of business school curricula

A few years ago a heading such as 'Are Business Schools Silent Partners in Corporate Crime?' (Swanson and Frederick 2003: 24) would have been unthinkable. During the past five years the international business world has been shocked at the revelation of unprecedented corporate misconduct and crime. For years there was not really any

---

1 This paper uses several extracts from articles published in the popular press. They are used to illustrate the concerns and views in popular culture on issues of corporate citizenship. The paper does not necessarily support the views held in the popular press. The quotations do, however, constitute a public debate outside the 'normal' corridors of the academe.

appetite to doubt the academic integrity and the way in which universities and business schools have been preparing business leaders. Now there is a growing suspicion that behind the crime and corruption may hide unbridled personal and corporate selfishness.

Mintzberg *et al.* (2002) add their voices to the debate to express their concerns about the 'selfishness' of corporate capitalism. In their article 'Beyond Selfishness' Mintzberg *et al.* explore the 'syndrome of selfishness, built on half-truths [that] has taken hold of our corporations, and our societies, as well as our minds'. They believe that '[t]his calculus of glorified self-interest and the fabrications upon which it is based must be challenged' (Mintzberg *et al.* 2002: 67). The writers investigate the dramatic extent to which selfishness has increased and coloured corporations' view of their responsibility to and role in society.

> A society devoid of selfishness is certainly difficult to imagine. But a society that glorifies selfishness can be imagined only as base. The intention here is to challenge such a society—not to deny human nature, but to correct a distorted view of it (Mintzberg *et al.* 2002: 67).

The authors continue to explore, among others, the following myths:

▶ 'We are all *Homo economicus*, obsessed with our self-interest, intent on maximising our personal gains' (Mintzberg *et al.* 2002: 68).

▶ 'Corporations exist to maximise shareholder value' (Mintzberg *et al.* 2002: 70).

▶ 'A rising tide of prosperity lifts all boats' (Mintzberg *et al.* 2002: 73).

The question that Swanson and Frederick (2003: 25) raise is to what extent business school curricula have caused and perpetuated this selfishness, greed and unethical behaviour. Issues of corporate citizenship, corporate governance and sustainable development are still strangers at the door (Springett and Kearins 2001: 213). Business school curricula are still shaped by market-driven values and goals, where issues such as corporate citizenship and sustainable development are not likely to be high on the agenda (Springett and Kearins 2001: 213; Swanson and Frederick 2003: 24).

This is about to change. During 2004 the European Foundation for Management Development (EFMD) and the United Nations Global Compact have started an initiative to develop a new generation of globally responsible leaders and managers. They have invited business schools and companies from all parts of the world to work together to re-imagine the role globally responsible business leaders can and should play. They will investigate current business school curricula and propose changes on a global scale that will be both enforceable and teachable. This initiative hopes to not only address concerns about the quality of business leadership in general but also to shape business leaders who take issues of corporate citizenship and sustainability seriously. 'Sustainability—in the sense of a system of deep-rooted justice and a fair and responsible allocation and use of ecological resources—requires a political philosophy adequate to its unique task of effecting change' (Tinker and Gray 2002: 727).

This paper proposes that. in re-imagining globally responsible business leadership, we have to take the paradoxes and 'grand narratives' of neocapitalism and consumerism seriously.

Exploring the paradoxes and grand narratives

Zadek (2001: 14) suggests that corporate citizenship has grown through three generations, each trying to answer a specific question. The first generation tackled the question: 'Can corporations be responsible in ways that do not detract from, and may add, commercial value to their business?' The answer was in the affirmative. The second generation asked: 'Are more responsible companies likely to prosper in the future?' Here, a less certain answer was provided. The present generation of corporate citizenship is confronted with the question: 'Is corporate citizenship likely to make a significant contribution to addressing the growing levels of poverty, exclusion and environmental degradation?' (Zadek 2001: 14). It is the consideration of this last question that should have the biggest impact on the success and reputation of corporate citizenship in Africa.

Corporate citizenship on the African continent is dealing with all three questions *at once*. This state of being 'on the edge of chaos' (Calton and Payne 2003) leads to the questioning of the basic notions of citizenship and profitability. Worldwide, companies are faced with an enormous task to balance the demands of all the stakeholders who either have an impact on the business sector or on which the business sector has an impact. Many critics view every move towards creating a business case as just another hidden agenda to 'cover up' for self-interest or an attempt to build loyalty, equity in integrity and support in times of need, which will necessarily be evident in the increase of the monetary value of the company. This self-interest of business is nowhere in more stark contrast to reality than on the African continent, where 300 million people in sub-Saharan Africa live on less than US$1 a day (Maharaj 2004: 14) and where this bleak situation is exposed daily with headlines such as 'Stark Poverty in a Sea of Oil and Diamonds' (Tleane 2003: 23).

Selfishness and profitability

Corporate citizenship appeals to the 'selfish' heart of business and urges it to take up its role as a responsible citizen in its respective communities. On the African continent this 'selfish heart of business' is at times more likely to be exposed as the 'heart of darkness' (with apologies to Joseph Conrad 1973). How else do you explain:

▶ That Africa is becoming the dumping site for second-hand clothing, 'polluting fridges and air-conditioners, expired medicines and old mattresses' (Maharaj 2004: 14) and waste (Ngobese 2004: 15)—including nuclear waste?

▶ Two hundred thousand children being exploited as cheap labour in West and Central Africa alone (Nkwanyane 2002: 30)?

▶ The living conditions of ordinary people in Angola, where the leaders (business and political) live a life of luxury (Tleane 2003: 23) amid a sea of oil and diamonds?

How to attain this crucial balance between self-interest and being a responsible citizen is a critical question in the debate on corporate citizenship in Africa. 'We either win this war to save our land, or we will be exterminated, because we have nowhere to run to' (Ken Saro-Wiwa, quoted by Ramsamy 2004: 8). A critical question that has to be raised and answered in the education of corporate citizenship is: 'Why do they get away with it?' In Europe certain practices would ruin a company's reputation beyond repair. In Africa hardly an eyebrow is raised.

Corporate citizenship today is faced again with the 'social must' (Thurrow, quoted by Birch 2001: 54). The 'must' part is, however, changing to going '*beyond* social responsibility'. Education will play an essential role in 'rethinking' corporate citizenship.

Questioning neocapitalism

The relationship between modern-day business and society is founded in capitalism, whether this is called global capitalism or neocapitalism. The gross inequality that is one of the characteristics of today's world is not simply a matter 'of the gap between rich and poor, but of the structural relationships in the economic arena of propertied and non-propertied segments of population' (Reitz 2004: 4). Education stands accused that it does not seriously intend to change society for the better of all, but rather intends to 'make the world safe for global capitalism' (McLaren 2000: 196). The Global Compact is accused of threatening to 'bring commercialism into the UN' (Martens 2004) and of increasing the power of transnational corporations in the UN (Richter 2003: 4). Educators are accused of being 'supplicants of corporate America and to work at the behest of the corporate bottom line' (McLaren 2000: 197).

Corporate citizenship and the teaching thereof has to take seriously the notion that 'human capital' has become 'traumatised capital' (McLaren 1994: 1) in an age where capitalism has become 'triumphant' (Zald 2001: 1). McLaren accuses capitalism of 'set[ting] the stage for the triumphant comeback of the dark ages of extreme poverty and institut[ing] a long and unendurable period of suffering and hopelessness for millions of the world population' (McLaren 1994: 2). 'Once considered the oxygen of democracy, capital now habitually blunts democracy, placing democracy at risk' (McLaren 1994: 9).

This warning is echoed by Hertz in her book *The Silent Takeover: Global Capitalism and the Death of Democracy* (2003). While the evidence against corporate capitalism is rife, there are also attempts to sell 'compassionate capitalism' and responsible capitalism (Devos and Devos 1994; Benioff and Southwick 2004). Majakathata Mokoena (2002: 2) forwards the notion that we should 'blame the capitalists, not capitalism, for Africa's woes'. A critical corporate citizenship education will have to scrutinise the development and history of capitalism in Africa to disentangle a possible legitimate economic dispensation and philosophy from its legacy, which is tainted by colonialism, the slave trade and apartheid.

Efforts to curb 'triumphant' or 'rampant' capitalism include legislation and rewarding good corporate citizenship. An example of the latter is the launch of the Johannesburg Securities Exchange (JSE) Socially Responsible Investment (SRI) Index in South Africa in 2004. It signals a strong institutional intent on the part of the JSE to transform the South African business landscape.[2] However, what remains a challenge is not only to change society's dependence on regulations, codes and indexes to fast-track socio-economic transformation but also to encourage the acceptance of personal responsibility to challenge the known order of business (responsible versus triumphant capitalism).

The enchantment of consumerism

Sensation and spectacle find willing consumers, more than critical and open debate does. In the postmodern era, life has become a spectacle (Firat and Venkatesh 1995: 251) where goods have become more than their specific content, where they have become 'messages', 'visible statements' (Douglas and Isherwood 1996: ix) and 'symbols' (Baudrillard 1981). For those living on the edges, brands such as Nike, Levi's and BMW are much more than brands—they allow them into the life of the rich and famous (Rory 2004: 40-41).

Up to now business school curricula have not required of their learners to investigate these 'grand narratives' (Lyotard 1984: 40) of consumerism and 'life as spectacle' (Firat and Venkatesh 1995: 251). While such criticality may be a luxury in the northern hemisphere, it is of crucial importance on the African continent. The successful selling

---

2 A study by de Jongh (2003) set out to determine indicators of corporate social performance in South Africa. In the findings of the study, the following groups of indicators were suggested: compliance, corporate governance, stakeholder engagement, social development contributions, integration, employee welfare, reputation, sustainability, contextual, and standard setting.

of the 'great American dream' is visible throughout the African continent, where consumers who have difficulty surviving at the same time aspire to have Nikes, Levi's and a pair of Police sunglasses, such as those sported by their heroes on television programmes. When the 'grand narrative' is a celebration of luxury and indulgence, it is but a short shift to accepting that the end justifies the means.

Critical corporate citizenship education

On the one hand there is a call for more codes of ethics and stricter legislation to regulate the relations of business in society, while others see teaching and training as the *only* viable strategy to curb the tide of abuse (Lampe and Finn 1994: 120; Armstrong *et al.* 2003: 1; Prozesky 2003). If the cynical view adopted by Tipgos is true, however, *any* strategy would be worthless: 'Management fraud is unstoppable because no controls, past or present, exist to completely control management's actions' (Tipgos 2002: 34). Furthermore, how does one counter a culture where 'anything goes as long as it makes money' (Hatcher 2003a: 44)? Yet, as Prinsloo and Beukes indicated, the question that really creates cause for concern is: '*What's wrong* with the notion that anything goes as long as it makes money?' (Prinsloo and Beukes 2004: 8). The authors investigated the powerful effect that popular culture and consumerism has on the choices business leaders and corporations make. The notion that 'anything goes as long as it makes more money' is contributing to the tainted relationship between corporations and the communities in which they operate.

In light of the above, we would like to propose that we urgently need alternative approaches to teaching corporate citizenship that affects business and society.

Towards a critical corporate citizenship pedagogy

Should curricula take the paradoxical nature of corporate governance and citizenship in a postmodern society seriously, then a curriculum may resemble 'a pluralist sense-making process for addressing messy problems' (Calton and Payne 2003: 7). Critical curriculum theories acknowledge reality as 'a mixture of the complex, the temporal and the multiple' (Prigogine and Stengers 1984, quoted by Doll 1986: 13). In order to critically and effectively address the paradoxes at the 'edge of chaos', we need to move away from a measured, linear curriculum to a 'transformatory' curriculum (Doll 1986: 13).

Although Prigogine and Stengers's publication contributed to a fresh understanding and rationale for 'transformatory' education, the concept of education as a transformatory and liberating process is supported and explored by a variety of authors and educators. Paulo Freire is most probably best known for proposing a *Pedagogy for Liberation* (1987) and expounding on *Education, the Practice of Freedom* (1976). Mezirow wrote on 'learning as transformation' (2000), Giroux on education as 'rage and hope'[3] and Simon on a 'pedagogy of possibility' (1987).

A critical pedagogy differs dramatically from present teaching practice, which in general resembles what Freire called 'banking education' (in Giroux 1983: 284). Freire compared traditional education to a banking process: the teacher 'deposits' the knowledge in the learners.

> Instead of communicating, the teacher issues communiqués and makes deposits which the students patiently receive, memorise and repeat. This is the 'banking' concept of

---

3 www.perfectfit.org/CT/giroux1.html

education, in which the scope of action allowed to the students extends only as far as receiving, filing, and storing deposits (Freire in Giroux 1983: 284).

Transformatory education has as its starting point that 'for learners to change their meaning schemes (specific beliefs, attitudes, and emotional reactions) they must engage in critical reflection on their experiences, which in turn leads to a perspective transformation' (Mezirow 1991: 167). So far we have indicated that the 'grand narratives' of corporate capitalism and consumerism have to be engaged with and analysed in order to confront learners with the possibility that there might also be *other* narratives which should be heard. This will require of learners to be confronted with 'disorienting dilemmas' (Mezirow 1991: 167) which, as they reflect on all the narratives and voices, may lead to a transformation of perspective. Learners have to discover the 'hidden' curriculum behind corporate citizenship education and discover that business school syllabuses are not neutral. Every curriculum always has 'moral and political dimensions' (Simon 1987: 312).

Giroux has explored education as a political, socioeconomic and culturally tainted action in a number of works (1983, 1997, 2000). He and others (for example, McLaren) have developed a theory of 'critical' and 'insurgent ' multiculturalism to address the incompetence of multicultural education in the United States of America. The failure of multicultural education to effectively deal with the inequalities of the respective communities and society in general has caused a rethink on the nature of education. It was found that teaching 'tolerance' does not change society for the better (Prinsloo and Beukes 2004).

In the teaching of corporate citizenship, the pedagogy underlying the teaching will have to take cognisance of the fact that '[d]ifference is *always* a product of history, power and ideology' (Giroux 2000: 199; our emphasis). Because corporate citizenship is embedded in the relations of political and economic power in society, the only education that would be a responsible approach would be one of 'critique and possibility' (Giroux 2000: 196); or, as Giroux's web page indicates, '[r]age and [h]ope'.[4]

For education to effectively address and confront the often paradoxical nature of corporate citizenship, learners will have to be sensitised to become 'enraged' in order to 'hope'. Teaching learners the market and capital values of 'compassionate capitalism' will not eradicate the basic inequalities and metanarratives guiding the relationship between business and society. Most educational programmes sell the current hegemonial metanarratives to learners to participate uncritically in a society driven by 'triumphant capitalism' (Zald 2001).

Reflection as critical methodology

In order to provide society with *reflective* and *critical* managers (Mintzberg 2004: 28), we need 'third-generation management development'. Mintzberg's (2004: 33) proposal starts with 'managing the self—the reflective mindset'. The manager as reflective practitioner stands at the centre of a new approach to teaching corporate citizenship. This 'alternate criticality' involves certain logical and analytical skills that assist the learner to 'think outside a framework of conventional understandings; it means to think anew, *to think differently*' (Burbules and Berk 1999: 59).

A more critical approach to teaching corporate citizenship will have to reflect seriously on the history of the social and political nature of existing relations and canons of knowledge.

---

4 See footnote 3.

> Not only organisational behaviour and organisational theory, but accounting, financial economics, and marketing deal with historically embedded, culturally configured, socially constructed institutions and practices. While professional schools must teach best current practices and understandings, by showing where those practices and understandings come from, they will provide tools for understanding the next generation of practices (Zald 2001: 12).

Within the African context, where nations and individuals still engage with the legacies of colonialism and apartheid, learners should be encouraged to explore new ways of being. Naidoo (2004: 2) petitions for a return to African values. 'Ubuntu',[5] the view that human beings co-exist and are interdependent, serves as a spiritual foundation of many African societies, emphasising the collective good of society over that of the individual (Naidoo 2004: 2). Ubuntu is further hailed as a possible 'counterpoint to the extractive capitalist model' (Nussbaum 2003: 1).[6]

Conclusion

Corporate citizenship on the African continent faces many challenges that are also encountered globally. The paradoxes and history of this continent often require of corporations to operate 'on the edge of chaos' and within the 'messiness' of corruption, crime, poverty and the AIDS pandemic. The intense need Africa has for development and investment renders it prone to abuse and exploitation.

In this article we have explored the impotency of traditional business school curricula to prepare business leaders for the paradoxes and disarray of corporate citizenship. Present curricula may well perpetuate the 'grand narratives' of neocapitalism and selfishness.

A critical pedagogy provides corporate citizenship education in Africa with the necessary tools to critique, to search for new possibilities and to become engaged. The starting point is thinking anew.

Bibliography

Andriof, J., and M. McIntosh (eds.) (2001) *Perspectives on Corporate Citizenship* (Sheffield, UK: Greenleaf Publishing).

Armstrong, M.B., J.E. Ketz and D. Owsen (2003) 'Ethics Education in Accounting: Moving toward Ethical Motivation and Ethical Behaviour', *Journal of Accounting Education* 21: 1-16.

Baudrillard, J. (1981) *For a Critique of the Political Economy of the Sign* (St Louis, MO: Telos).

Benioff, M., and K. Southwick (2004) *Compassionate Capitalism: How Corporations Can Make Doing Good an Integral Part of Doing Well* (Franklin Lakes, NJ: Career Press).

Birch, D. (2001) 'Corporate Citizenship: Rethinking Business Beyond Corporate Social Responsibility', in J. Andriof and M. McIntosh (eds.), *Perspectives on Corporate Citizenship* (Sheffield, UK: Greenleaf Publishing): 53-65.

Bloch, E. (1970) *A Philosophy of the Future* (New York: Herder & Herder).

Burbules, N.C., and R. Berk (1999) 'Critical Thinking and Critical Pedagogy: Relations, Differences, and Limits', in T.S. Popkewitz and L. Fendler (eds.), *Critical Theories in Education* (New York: Routledge).

Calton, J.M., and S.L. Payne (2003) 'Coping with Paradox: Multistakeholder Learning Dialogue as a Pluralist Sensemaking Process for Addressing Messy Problems', *Business and Society* 42.1: 7-42.

Castells, M., R. Flecha, P. Freire, H.A. Giroux, D. Macedo and P. Willis (1994) *Critical Education in the New Information Age* (Lanham, MD: Rowman & Littlefield).

---

5 'Ubuntu' is an African concept stating 'I am a human being because of you'.
6 The extent to which the new emphasis on 'ubuntu' will have an impact on the 'grand narrative' of neocapitalism will have to be seen.

Conrad, J. (1973) *The Heart of Darkness* (London: Penguin).

De Jongh, D. (2003) *Indicators of Corporate Social Performance in South Africa* (doctoral dissertation; Pretoria: University of Pretoria, Faculty of Economic and Management Sciences, Department of Communication Management).

Devos, R.M., and R. Devos (1994) *Compassionate Capitalism* (Muskegon, MI: Plume).

Doll, E. (1986) 'Prigogine: A New Sense of Order, a New Curriculum', *Theory into Practice* 25.1: 10-16.

Donaldson, T., and T.W. Dunfee (1994) 'Towards a Unified Conception of Business Ethics: Integrative Social Contracts Theory', *Academy of Management Review* 19.2: 252-84.

Douglas, M., and B. Isherwood (1996) *The World of Goods: Towards an Anthropology of Consumption* (New York: Routledge).

Firat, A.F., and A. Venkatesh (1995) 'Liberatory Postmodernism and the Reenchantment of Consumption', *Journal of Consumer Research* 22.3: 239-67.

Freire, P. (1976) *Education, the Practice of Freedom* (London: Writers' and Readers' Cooperative).

—— (1987) *Pedagogy for Liberation* (Granby, MA: Bergin & Garvey).

—— (1989) *Learning to Question: A Pedagogy of Liberation* (Geneva: World Council of Churches).

Giroux, H.A. (1983) *Theory and Resistance in Education: A Pedagogy for the Opposition* (South Hadley, MA: Bergin & Garvey).

—— (1997) 'Insurgent Multiculturalism and the Promise of Pedagogy', in A.H. Halsley, H. Lauder, P. Brown and A.S. Wells (eds.), *Education: Culture, Economy, Society* (New York: Oxford University Press): 113-30.

—— (2000) 'Crossing the Boundaries of Educational Discourse: Modernism, Postmodernism and Feminism', in E.M. Duarte and S. Smith (eds.), *Foundational Perspectives in Multicultural Education* (New York: Longman): 195-212.

——, C. Lankshear, P. McLaren and M. Peters (1996) *Counternarratives: Cultural Studies and Critical Pedagogies in Postmodern Spaces* (New York: Routledge).

Grayson, D., and A. Hodges (2004) *Corporate Social Opportunity: Seven Steps to Make Corporate Social Responsibility Work for Your Business* (Sheffield, UK: Greenleaf Publishing).

Halsley, A.H., H. Lauder, P. Brown and A.S. Wells (eds.) (1997) *Education. Culture, Economy, Society* (New York: Oxford University Press).

Hatcher, T. (2003a) 'New World Ethics', *TD*, August 2003: 42-47.

—— (2003b) 'Ethical Compass', *Executive Excellence*, July 2003: 19.

Hertz, N. (2003) *The Silent Takeover: Global Capitalism and the Death of Democracy* (London: HarperCollins).

Jennings, M.M. (2002) 'The Critical Role of Ethics', *Internal Auditor*, December 2002: 46-51.

Lampe, J.C., and D.W. Finn (1994) 'Teaching Ethics in Accounting Curricula', *Business and Professional Ethics Journal* 13.1–2: 89-128.

Lister, D. (2004) 'Equatorial Guinea's Oil Boom Benefits Few', *This Day*, 1 September 2004: 4.

Lyotard, J.F. (1984) *The Postmodern Condition* (Minneapolis, MN: University of Minneapolis Press).

Maharaj, D. (2004) 'Africa on $1 a Day', *Sunday Independent*, 15 August 2004: 14.

Martens, J. (2004) 'Precarious "Partnerships": Six Problems of the Global Compact between Business and the UN', www.globalpolicy.org/reform/business/2004/0623partnerships.htm, 28 September 2004.

McLaren, P. (1994) 'Introduction. Traumatizing Capital: Oppositional Pedagogies in the Age of Consent', in M. Castells, R. Flecha, P. Freire, H.A. Giroux, D. Macedo and P. Willis (eds.), *Critical Education in the New Information Age* (New York: Rowman & Littlefield).

—— (1997) 'Multiculturalism and the Postmodern Critique: Toward a Pedagogy of Resistance and Transformation', in A.H. Halsley, H. Lauder, P. Brown and A.S. Wells (eds.), *Education: Culture, Economy, Society* (New York: Oxford University Press): 520-40.

—— (2000) *Che Guevara, Paulo Freire, and the Pedagogy of Revolution* (New York: Lanham, Boulder).

Mezirow, J. (1991) *Transformative Dimensions of Adult Learning* (Oxford, UK: Jossey-Bass).

—— (1995) 'Transformation Theory of Adult Learning', in M.R. Welton (ed.), *In Defense of the Lifeworld: Critical Perspectives on Adult Learning* (New York: Suny).

Mezirow, J. (2000) *Learning as Transformation: Critical Perspectives on a Theory in Progress* (San Francisco: Jossey-Bass).

Mintzberg, H. (2004) 'Third-Generation Management', *TD*, March 2004: 28-37.

——, R. Simons and K. Basu (2002) 'Beyond Selfishness', *MIT Sloan Management Review*, Fall 2002: 67-74.

Mokoena, M. (2002) 'Blame the Capitalists, Not Capitalism, for Africa's Woes', *City Press*, 2 June 2002: 2.

Naidoo, R. (2004) 'A Return to African Values', *Business Day*, 13 April 2004: 2.

Ngobese, Z. (2004) 'Environmental Crime Feels Sting of Green Scorpions', *Star*, 14 January 2004: 15.

Nkomo, S. (2003) 'Teaching Business Ethically in the "New" South Africa', *Management Communication Quarterly* 17.1: 128-35.

Nkwanyane, T. (2002) 'Child Labour Rife in SA', *City Press*, 10 February 2002: 30.

Nussbaum, B. (2003) 'Ubuntu and Business . . . Reflections and Questions', *World Business Academy* 17.3: 2-16.

Popkewitz, T.S., and L. Fendler (eds.) (1999) *Critical Theories in Education* (New York: Routledge).

Prigogine, L., and I. Stengers (1984) *Order Out of Chaos* (New York: Bantam).

Prinsloo, P., and C. Beukes (2004) 'It's Not on Top, It's Inside' (unpublished article).

Prozesky, M. (2003) 'Ethics Education in the Accountancy Profession', *Accountancy SA*, June 2003: 2-5.

Ramsamy, D. (2004) 'Just Visiting', *Independent on Saturday*, 1 May 2004: 8.

Reitz, C. (2004) 'Teaching about Oppression and Exploitation: Critical Theory and the Origins of Inequality', eserver.org/clogic/2004/reitz.html, 28 September 2004.

Richter, J. (2003) *Building on Quicksand: The Global Compact, Democratic Governance and Nestlé* (Geneva: CETIM, IBFAN/GIFA and Berne Declaration).

Rory, C. (2004) 'Driving the Black Man's Wish in a Very White Economy', *Mail and Guardian*, 16 April 2004: 40-41.

Simon, R. (1987) 'Empowerment as a Pedagogy of Possibility', *Language Arts* 64.4: 370-83.

Springett, D., and K. Kearins (2001) 'Gaining Legitimacy? Sustainable Development in Business School Curricula', *Sustainable Development* 9: 213-21.

Swanson, D.L., and W.C. Frederick (2003) 'Are Business Schools Silent Partners in Corporate Crime?', *Journal of Corporate Citizenship* 9 (Spring 2003): 24-27.

Tinker, T., and B. Gray (2002) 'Beyond a Critique of Reason: From Policy to Politics to Praxis in Environmental and Social Research', *Accounting, Auditing and Accountability Journal* 16.5: 727-61.

Tipgos, M.A. (2002) 'Why Management Fraud is Unstoppable', *The CPA Journal*, December 2002: 34-41.

Tleane, C. (2003) 'Stark Poverty in a Sea of Oil and Diamonds', *City Press*, 26 October 2003: 23.

Welton, M.R. (ed.) (1995) *In Defense of the Lifeworld* (New York: Suny).

Willmott, H. (1992) *Critical Management Studies* (London: Sage).

Zadek, S. (2001) *Third Generation Corporate Citizenship* (London: The Foreign Policy Centre).

—— (2004) 'Responsible Competitiveness: Scaling Up Corporate Responsibility', Powerpoint presentation (personal communication).

Zald, M.N. (2001) 'Spinning Disciplines: Critical Management Studies in the Context of the Transformation of Management Education', plenary address, *Critical Management Studies Workshop*, Washington, DC, 4 August 2001.

Epilogue

The Campaign to Make Poverty History

Nelson Mandela

I am privileged to be here today at the invitation of the Campaign to Make Poverty History.

As you know, I recently formally announced my retirement from public life and should really not be here.

However, as long as poverty, injustice and gross inequality persist in our world, none of us can truly rest.

Moreover, the Global Campaign for Action Against Poverty represents such a noble cause that we could not decline the invitation.

Massive poverty and obscene inequality are such terrible scourges of our times—times in which the world boasts breathtaking advances in science, technology, industry and wealth accumulation—that they have to rank alongside slavery and apartheid as social evils.

The Global Campaign for Action Against Poverty can take its place as a public movement alongside the movement to abolish slavery and the international solidarity against apartheid.

And I can never thank the people of Britain enough for their support through those days of the struggle against apartheid. Many stood in solidarity with us, just a few yards from this spot.

Through your will and passion, you assisted in consigning that evil system forever to history. But, in this new century, millions of people in the world's poorest countries remain imprisoned, enslaved, and in chains.

They are trapped in the prison of poverty. It is time to set them free.

Like slavery and apartheid, poverty is not natural. It is man-made and it can be overcome and eradicated by the actions of human beings.

And overcoming poverty is not a gesture of charity. It is an act of justice. It is the protection of a fundamental human right, the right to dignity and a decent life.

While poverty persists, there is no true freedom.

The steps that are needed from the developed nations are clear. The first is ensuring trade justice.

I have said before that trade justice is a truly meaningful way for the developed countries to show commitment to bringing about an end to global poverty.

The second is an end to the debt crisis for the poorest countries. The third is to deliver much more aid and make sure it is of the highest quality.

In 2005, there is a unique opportunity for making an impact.

In September, world leaders will gather in New York to measure progress since they made the Millennium Declaration in the year 2000.

That declaration promised to halve extreme poverty.

But, at the moment, the promise is falling tragically behind. Those leaders must now honour their promises to the world's poorest citizens.

Tomorrow, here in London, the G7 finance ministers can make a significant beginning. I am happy to have been invited to meet with them.

The G8 leaders, when they meet in Scotland in July, have already promised to focus on the issue of poverty, especially in Africa.

I say to all those leaders: do not look the other way; do not hesitate. Recognise that the world is hungry for action, not words. Act with courage and vision.

I am proud to wear the symbol of this global call to action in 2005. This white band is from my country.

In a moment, I want to give this band to you—young people of Britain—and ask you to take it forward along with millions of others to the G8 summit in July.

I entrust it to you. I will be watching with anticipation.

We thank you for coming here today. Sometimes it falls upon a generation to be great. You can be that great generation. Let your greatness blossom.

Of course, the task will not be easy. But not to do this would be a crime against humanity, against which I ask all humanity now to rise up.

Make Poverty History in 2005. Make History in 2005. Then we can all stand with our heads held high.

Thank you.

Source: Nelson Mandela, speech in London's Trafalgar Square for the campaign to end poverty in the developing world, 3 February 2005

Diary of Events

September–December 2005

A selective listing of key conferences, seminars and exhibitions in the field of corporate responsibility

16 September 2005   Nottingham, UK

Business, Government and CSR: Redefining Boundaries and Responsibilities

iccsr@nottingham.ac.uk

---

19 September 2005   New York, USA

7th Annual Conference
Beyond Compliance: Innovative Strategies for Responsible Sourcing

Lisa Bernstein   +212 684 1414 ext. 204   LBernstein@sa-intl.org
www.sa-intl.org/Training%20and%20Programs/Conferences.htm

18–19 October 2005   London, UK

The New Role for Business in Developing Countries

Laura Geron   +44 (0) 207 375 7226   +49 (0)89 289 24805   laura.geron@ethicalcorp.com
www.ethicalcorp.com

25–26 October 2005   New York, USA

A World of Risk. A World of Opportunities?

roundtable@unepfi.org   www.unepfi.org/events/2005/roundtable

---

1–4 November 2005   Washington, DC, USA

BSR 2005 Annual Conference
Questioning Assumptions: Changing Frameworks

BSR, 111 Sutter Street, 12th Floor, San Francisco, CA 94104, USA   +1 415 984 3200   +1 415 984 3201
www.bsr.org/BSRConferences/2005/index.cfm

2–4 November 2005   Frankfurt, Germany

7th Annual Triple Bottom Line Investing (TBLI) Conference

📞 +31 (0)20 4286752   💻 gabrielle@tbli.org   ⊕ www.tbli.org/content/conf_program.html

---

 2–3 December 2005   Berlin, Germany

'International Organisations and Global Environmental Governance': 2005 Berlin Conference on the Human Dimensions of Global Environmental Change

⊕ www.fu-berlin.de/ffu/akumwelt/bc2005/index.html

 5–6 December 2005   Warsaw, Poland

4th EABIS Colloquium 2005
Corporate Responsibility and Competitiveness: Developing Human Capital for Sustainable Growth

👤 Dr Boleslaw Rok   💻 brok@wspiz.edu.pl   ⊕ www.eabis.org

About the Journal of Corporate Citizenship

THE JOURNAL OF CORPORATE CITIZENSHIP (JCC) is a multidisciplinary peer-reviewed journal that focuses on integrating theory about corporate citizenship with management practice. It provides a forum in which the tensions and practical realities of making corporate citizenship real can be addressed in a reader-friendly, yet conceptually and empirically rigorous format.

JCC aims to publish *the best ideas integrating the theory and practice of corporate citizenship in a format that is readable, accessible, engaging, interesting and useful* for readers in its already wide audience in business, consultancy, government, NGOs and academia. It encourages practical, theoretically sound, and (when relevant) empirically rigorous manuscripts that address real-world implications of corporate citizenship in global and local contexts. Topics related to corporate citizenship can include (but are not limited to): corporate responsibility, stakeholder relationships, public policy, sustainability and environment, human and labour rights/ issues, governance, accountability and transparency, globalisation, small and medium-sized enterprises (SMEs) as well as multinational firms, ethics, measurement, and specific issues related to corporate citizenship, such as diversity, poverty, education, information, trust, supply chain management, and problematic or constructive corporate/human behaviours and practices.

In addition to articles linking the theory and practice of corporate citizenship, JCC also encourages innovative or creative submissions (for peer review). Innovative submissions can highlight issues of corporate citizenship from a critical perspective, enhance practical or conceptual understanding of corporate citizenship, or provide new insights or alternative perspectives on the realities of corporate citizenship in today's world. Innovative submissions might include: critical perspectives and controversies, photography, essays, poetry, drama, reflections, and other innovations that help bring corporate citizenship to life for management practitioners and academics alike.

JCC welcomes contributions from researchers and practitioners involved in any of the areas mentioned above. Manuscripts should be written so that they are comprehensible to an intelligent reader, avoiding jargon, formulas and extensive methodological treatises wherever possible. They should use examples and illustrations to highlight the ideas, concepts and practical implications of the ideas being presented. Theory is important and necessary; but theory—with the empirical research and conceptual work that supports theory—needs to be balanced by integration into practices to stand the tests of time and usefulness. JCC aims to be the premier journal to publish articles on corporate citizenship that accomplish this integration of theory and practice. We want the journal to be read as much by executives leading corporate citizenship as it is by academics seeking sound research and scholarship.

JCC appears quarterly and the contents of each issue include: editorials; peer-reviewed papers by leading writers; a global digest of key initiatives and developments from the previous quarter; reviews; case studies; think-pieces; and an agenda of conferences and meetings. A key feature is the 'Turning Points' section. Turning Points are commentaries, controversies, new ideas, essays and insights that aim to be provocative and engaging, raise the important issues of the day and provide observations on what is too new yet to be the subject of empirical and theoretical studies. JCC continues to produce occasional issues dedicated to a single theme. These have included 'Corporate Transparency, Accountability and Governance', 'Stakeholder Responsibility' and 'The Global Compact'; forthcoming special issues will focus on, among others, 'Corporate Citizenship in Latin America and the Caribbean'.

EDITOR

David Birch, Director, Corporate Citizenship Research Unit, Deakin University, 221 Burwood Highway, Melbourne, Victoria, Australia 3125; email: edjcc@bc.edu.

Regional Editors:

North American Editor: Sandra Waddock, Professor of Management, Boston College, Carroll School of Management, Senior Research Fellow, Center for Corporate Citizenship, Chestnut Hill, MA 02467 USA; tel: +1 617 552 0477; fax: +1 617 552 0433; email: waddock@bc.edu

Euro-Africa Editor: Malcolm McIntosh, Department of Economics and International Development, University of Bath, 242 Bloomfield Road, Bath BA2 2AX, UK; email: malcolm.mcintosh@btinternet.com.

Notes for Contributors

SUBMISSIONS
Submissions via email (edjcc@bc.edu) are preferred if saved as Microsoft Word or RTF documents. Alternatively, two copies of the paper and a PC-compatible disk should be sent to: *Journal of Corporate Citizenship* Editorial Office, Boston College Center for Corporate Citizenship, Carroll School of Management, Chestnut Hill, MA 02467, USA; tel: +1 617 552 0477; fax: +1 617 552 0433; email: edjcc@bc.edu. Hard copies of all figures and tables will be required if the paper is accepted.

PRESENTATION
Articles should be 4,000–6,000 words long. Manuscripts should be arranged in the following order of presentation.

First page: Title, subtitle (if any), author's name, affiliation, full postal address and telephone, fax and email. Respective affiliations, addresses and emails of co-authors should be clearly indicated. Please also include approximately 50 words of biographical information on all authors, and a good-quality photograph of each (digital files should be at least 300 dpi × 3 cm; otherwise include a print [not transparency]).

Second page: A self-contained abstract of up to 150 words summarising the paper and its conclusions; and between 7 and 10 keywords, which will reflect the core themes of the paper (anticipating possible search terms that might be used by a potential reader).

Subsequent pages: Main body of text; footnotes/endnotes; list of references; appendices; tables; illustrations.

Authors are urged to write as concisely as possible, but not at the expense of clarity. The main title of the article should be kept short, up to 40 characters including spaces, but may be accompanied by a subtitle if further clarification is desired. Descriptive or explanatory passages, intrinsically necessary but which tend to break the flow of the main text, should be expressed as footnotes or appendices.

REFERENCES
All bibliographic references must be complete, comprising: authors and initials, full title and subtitle, place of publication, publisher, date, and page references. References to journal articles must include the volume and number of the journal and page extent. The layout should adhere to the following convention:

Clifton, R., and N. Buss (1992) 'Greener Communications', in M. Charter (ed.), *Greener Marketing: A Responsible Approach to Business* (Sheffield, UK: Greenleaf Publishing): 241-53.

Porter, M.E., and C. van der Linde (1995) 'Green and Competitive: Ending the Stalemate', *Harvard Business Review* 73.5 (September/October 1995): 120-33.

WCED (World Commission on Environment and Development) (1987) *Our Common Future* ('The Brundtland Report'; Oxford, UK: Oxford University Press).

These should be listed, alphabetically by author surname, at the end of the article. When citing, please use the 'author–date' method in parentheses, e.g. '(Ditz *et al.* 1995: 107)'.

ENDNOTES/FOOTNOTES
Endnotes/footnotes should be numbered consecutively in Arabic numerals and placed at the end of the manuscript before any figures. Automatic endnotes/footnotes are acceptable if using Microsoft Word.

TABLES, GRAPHS, ETC.
All tables, graphs, diagrams and other drawings should be clearly referred to and numbered consecutively in Arabic numerals. Their position should be indicated in the text. All figures must have captions. In all figures taken or adapted from other sources, a brief note to that effect is obligatory, below the caption.

PHOTOGRAPHS
Photographic material relevant to the article is encouraged and should be supplied at approx. 300 dpi × 7 cm, or as prints (not transparencies).

PROOFS
Authors are responsible for ensuring that all manuscripts (whether original or revised) are accurately typed before final submission. One set of proofs will be sent to authors before publication, which must be returned promptly.

▶ **To discuss ideas for contributions**, please contact the General Editor: David Birch, Director, Corporate Citizenship Research Unit, Deakin University, 221 Burwood Highway, Melbourne, Victoria, Australia 3125; email: birchd@deakin.edu.au.